Bill VanPatten, Michael J. Lesser, Gregory D. Keating

LIGHTS, CAMERA, SPANISH!

Pop in the movie. Learn the language.

McGraw Hill

New York   Chicago   San Francisco   Lisbon   London   Madrid   Mexico City
Milan   New Delhi   San Juan   Seoul   Singapore   Sydney   Toronto

1 2 3 4 5 6 7 8 9 10 11 12 13 14 15 16 17 18 19   DOC/DOC   0 9 8 7 6

ISBN-13: 978-0-07-147902-8 (book and DVD)
ISBN-10:   0-07-147902-3
ISBN-13: 978-0-07-148552-4 (book alone)
ISBN-10:   0-07-148552-X

Library of Congress Control Number: 2006924889

McGraw-Hill books are available at special quantity discounts to use as premiums and sales promotions, or for use in corporate training programs. For more information, please write to the Director of Special Sales, Professional Publishing, McGraw-Hill, Two Penn Plaza, New York, NY 10121-2298. Or contact your local bookstore.

This book is printed on acid-free paper.

Contents

Preface   v

PRÓLOGO: LOS ESPÍRITUS   1

EPISODIO 1: LA LLEGADA   5
   A primera vista   6
   A segunda vista   9
   Para escribir   10

EPISODIO 2: EL ENCUENTRO   13
   A primera vista   14
   A segunda vista   17
   Para escribir   18

EPISODIO 3: A LA VIÑA   21
   A primera vista   22
   A segunda vista   25
   Para escribir   26

EPISODIO 4: OTRO ENCUENTRO   29
   A primera vista   30
   A segunda vista   33
   Para escribir   34

EPISODIO 5: UN DÍA PERFECTO   37
   A primera vista   38
   A segunda vista   40
   Para escribir   42

EPISODIO 6: CONFRONTACIÓN   45
   A primera vista   46
   A segunda vista   49
   Para escribir   50

EPISODIO 7: BAJO EL SOL   53

A primera vista   54

A segunda vista   57

Para escribir   58

EPISODIO 8: SIN ALTERNATIVA   61

A primera vista   62

A segunda vista   65

Para escribir   66

EPISODIO 9: UN BRINDIS POR EL FUTURO   69

A primera vista   70

A segunda vista   73

Para escribir   74

Answer Key   77

Spanish-English Vocabulary   81

Preface

Are you tired of memorization? Do you feel that fill-in-the-blank just doesn't help you learn to listen to and speak Spanish? Welcome to *Lights, Camera, Spanish*, a unique guide to learning Spanish. The purpose of this program is to help readers who have some beginning level of Spanish advance to greater degrees of proficiency with the language. The centerpiece of this program is *Sol y viento*, a film designed specifically for language learners. *Sol y viento* consistently and constantly provides you with authentic samples of Spanish as you immerse yourself in the film's intriguing story. The activities and review material in this book will help to increase your comprehension, which in turn will help you to acquire more Spanish.

Sol y viento: The Film (I)

A successful young businessman gets orders to travel abroad to secure a land deal. Occupied with other matters and unwilling to go at first, he finally accepts the assignment and soon finds himself in Chile, a country far from his native California. Here, in this Andean nation—land of fertile valleys and soaring mountains, home to the condor, a place exotic and familiar all at once—this young man regains and embraces values he had set aside years ago. He rediscovers the importance of loyalty to family and friends and learns that a person's past is part of his or her soul. He rediscovers the meaning of community and how people and their land may share a bond as strong as that between any two people. Most importantly, he comes to understand that from love, forgiveness is possible—but it is not easily dispensed. Forgiveness must be earned.

Such is the story of the exciting new movie, *Sol y viento*. Follow Jaime "James" Talavera on his unexpected journey of self-discovery. Along the way meet Mario, the talkative personal driver who becomes Jaime's first friend in a new land. Meet Carlos, the secretive administrator of the winery who is eager to sell his family's lands—and those of others. Meet doña Isabel, the matriarch of the Sol y viento winery, and don Paco, the friend of the family who travels from Mexico to aid doña Isabel as she faces a crisis that threatens to alter an entire community's way of life. Finally, meet the high-spirited María, the young woman who captures Jaime's heart and mind. However, their mutual attraction may prove to be fleeting if Jaime does not grapple with the moral issues that confront him. As events unfold and the forces of nature conspire to draw the characters together, Jaime is forced to make the most difficult decision of his life.

Sol y viento: The Film (II)

One of the central themes examined in *Sol y viento* is the interaction between the forces of nature in the everyday lives of people. In fact, the sun (**sol**) and wind (**viento**) each play crucial roles in the film, as if they were characters themselves. Thus, "Sol y viento" is not just the name of a family winery; it displays the embodiment of elements of nature that help move the plot along.

Cast of Characters

Jaime
A successful businessman from San Francisco, California, who travels to Chile to finalize a deal with the Sol y viento winery.

María
A Chilean university professor and anthropologist who has always let her head rule over her heart.

Carlos
Proprietor and administrator of the Sol y viento winery who is working on the deal with Jaime's company.

Isabel
Carlos' ailing mother and, with her now-deceased husband, original proprietor of Sol y viento.

Paco
An old family friend of Isabel, who is called away from his native Mexico to help his friend in a time of need.

Mario
A taxi driver in Jaime's employ during his stay in Chile.

Traimaqueo
The longtime foreman of
the Sol y viento winery.

Yolanda
Traimaqueo's wife and
Isabel's primary
caregiver.

Diego
María's student assistant
at the university and at
anthropological dig sites.

Who are the Mapuches?

Throughout the course of the film, *Sol y viento* touches upon the plight of the Mapuche people and their struggle to retain their ancestral lands and maintain harmony with the Earth. The Mapuches are an indigenous people whose roots are found in southern and south central Chile and date back to thousands of years before the Europeans' arrival in the Western Hemisphere. In Quechua, the language of the Mapuche, **mapu** means *land* and **che** means *people*, essentially making them "people of the land." This connection to the earth is deeply rooted in the spirit and culture of the Mapuche people.

Since the 1880s, when the nations of Chile and Argentina began to appropriate ancestral Mapuche lands, the Mapuches have strived to retain these lands and, later, to make their struggles known to the world at large. In *Sol y viento*, this struggle is shown by the attempt of outsiders to purchase Mapuche lands in order to build a large dam to flood the region and produce cheap hydroelectric power.

In her book *Mi país inventado*, the acclaimed Chilean writer Isabel Allende relates a real-life struggle that echoes this theme in the film:

Nuestros indios no pertenecían a una cultura espléndida, como los aztecas, mayas o incas; eran hoscos, primitivos, irascibles y poco numerosos, pero tan corajudos, que estuvieron en pie de guerra durante trescientos años, primero contra los colonizadores españoles y luego contra la república. Fueron pacificados en 1880 y no se oyó hablar mucho de ellos por más de un siglo, pero ahora los mapuches —«gente de la tierra»— han vuelto a la lucha para defender las pocas tierras que les quedan, amenazadas por la construcción de una represa en el río Bío Bío.*

---

*Our Indians didn't belong to a grand culture, like the Aztecs, Mayas, or Incas; they were gruff, primitive, irritable, and few in number, but so brave that they waged war for 300 years, first against the Spanish settlers and then against the republic. They were pacified in 1880, and for more than a century you didn't hear a lot about them. But now the Mapuches —people of the earth— have renewed their fight in order to defend the few lands they have left, threatened by the construction of a dam on the Bío Bío River.
(Isabel Allende, *Mi país inventado* [Buenos Aires: Sudamericana, 2003], 56.)

One of the Mapuche characters in the film, the **machi,** is a spiritual leader of her tribe. At the beginning of the film, we see her telling a tale to a group of adults and children. As her tale unfolds, we witness how the lives of Jaime, María, and others are intricately woven into her story and how the forces of nature conspire to bring resolution to the conflicts with which they are faced.

The figurine seen here is a representation of a protective spirit in the beliefs of the Mapuche people. This spirit also plays an important role in the film, as you will see.

The Structure of the Viewer's Guide

The Viewer's Guide is designed to facilitate your comprehension of the film and to provide additional opportunities to increase proficiency in Spanish.

Dramatic and engaging, the *Sol y viento* film serves as the centerpiece for the Viewer's Guide. Divided into ten "episodes," consisting of a prologue and nine segments of approximately ten minutes each, the movie is easily viewed in short segments to maximize your new Spanish skills.

With the exception of the brief **Prólogo,** each episode is organized as follows:

A primera vista: These activities support a first viewing of the episode.

- **Antes de ver el episodio:** In this pre-viewing section, you will complete a wide variety of activity types, such as reviewing material from previous episodes, learning and practicing unfamiliar vocabulary from the episode, and guessing what may happen in the story. It is important for you to complete these activities as they will greatly enhance your initial viewing experience of the episode.

- **Después de ver el episodio:** After having watched the episode, you will complete a number of comprehension activities, including the guessing of unfamiliar words or phrases in context and a cloze passage that provides a brief summary of what happened in the episode, among others.

A segunda vista: These activities support a second viewing of the episode.

- **Antes de ver el episodio:** Upon a second viewing of the episode, you will be asked to listen for specific information to help you better understand the characters and the story line.

- **Después de ver el episodio:** After having watched the episode for a second time, you will work with activities that will push you to a higher level of understanding of the episode and will also demand more language production from you. You may watch the episode as many times as you like in order to complete these activites—in fact, the more you watch the same episode, the more Spanish you will learn.

Para escribir: To end each episode, you will complete a writing activity called **Para escribir.** Through a series of pre-writing and post-writing tasks you will explore the characters and their relationships in a much more profound way as you also improve your writing skills in Spanish.

Additional Features

Here are some additional features that are found in every episode of the Viewer's Guide.

- **Para pensar...** appears on every episode-opening page, along with stills from the film. Questions about the images encourage you to think about the upcoming episode.

- **Nota sobre el lenguaje** features identify a particular grammar point that may or may not be familiar to you. The brief explanations and examples are designed to help you with language you may hear in the episode or to help you complete the activities that correspond to the episode. Topics include:

  Episodio 1: the verb **ir**
  Episodio 2: uses of **ser** and **estar**
  Episodio 3: **gustar** and object pronouns
  Episodio 4: the preterite tense
  Episodio 5: the imperfect tense
  Episodio 6: formal and informal commands
  Episodio 7: the present subjunctive
  Episodio 8: the present and past perfect
  Episodio 9: the future tense

- ***Sol y viento:* Enfoque cultural** sections explore a cultural point illustrated in the *Sol y viento* film.

- **Detrás de la cámara** boxes provide additional information not presented in the film, such as the characters' backgrounds, motivation, personalities, and so forth.

- An **Answer Key,** located at the back of the Viewer's Guide, provides answers to many of the activities so that you can check your work.

About the Authors

Bill VanPatten is Professor of Spanish and Second Language Acquisition at the University of Illinois at Chicago where he is also the Director of Spanish Basic Language. His areas of research are input and input processing in second language acquisition and the effects of formal instruction on acquisitional processes. He has published widely in the fields of second language acquisition and language teaching and is a frequent conference speaker and presenter. In addition to *Sol y viento,* he is also the lead author of *¿Sabías que... ?,* Fourth Edition (2004, McGraw-Hill) and *Vistazos,* Second Edition (2006, McGraw-Hill). He is also the lead author and designer of *Destinos* and co-author with James F. Lee of *Making Communicative Language Teaching Happen,* Second Edition (2003, McGraw-Hill). He is also the author of *Input Processing and Grammar Instruction: Theory and Research* (1996, Ablex/Greenwood) and *From Input to Output: A Teacher's Guide to Second Language Acquisition* (2003, McGraw-Hill), and he is the editor of *Processing Instruction: Theory, Research, and Commentary* (2004, Erlbaum). When not engaged in academic activities, he writes fiction and performs stand-up comedy.

Michael J. Leeser is Assistant Professor of Spanish in the Department of Modern Languages and Linguistics at Florida State University, where he is also Director of the Spanish Basic Language Program. Before joining the faculty at Florida State, he taught a wide range of courses at the secondary and postsecondary levels, including courses in Spanish language and Hispanic cultures, teacher preparation courses for secondary school teachers, and graduate courses in communicative language teaching and second language acquisition. He received his Ph.D. in Spanish (Second Language Acquisition and Teacher Education) from the University of Illinois at Urbana-Champaign in 2003. His research interests include input processing during second language reading as well as second language classroom interaction. His research has appeared in journals such as *Studies in Second Language Acquisition* and *Language Teaching Research.* He also co-authored the CD-ROM, along with Bill VanPatten and Mark Overstreet, for *¿Sabías que... ?,* Fourth Edition (2004, McGraw-Hill).

Gregory D. Keating will complete his Ph.D. in Hispanic Linguistics and Second Language Acquisition at the University of Illinois at Chicago in 2005. His areas of research include Spanish sentence processing, the role instruction plays in language acquisition, and the acquisition of Spanish syntax and vocabulary. His doctoral research explores the relationship between language processing and grammatical competence in the acquisition of Spanish gender agreement. He is a frequent presenter at conferences in the United States and Mexico. He is also a recipient of several teaching awards, including one from the University of Notre Dame, where he received his M.A. in Spanish Literature. In addition to teaching and research, he has supervised many language courses and teaching assistants and has assisted in the coordination of technology-enhanced lower-division Spanish language programs.

MAR CARIBE

OCÉANO ATLÁNTICO

Barranquilla
Maracaibo
Caracas
PANAMÁ
VENEZUELA
GUYANA
Medellín
Georgetown
Panamá
Paramaribo
Bogotá
Cayena
Cali
SURINAME
GUYANA FRANCESA
COLOMBIA
Río Orinoco
Quito
Ecuador
ECUADOR
Río Amazonas
Belém
Guayaquil
Manaus
PERÚ
BRASIL
Recife
Cuzco
Lima
Brasília
Arequipa
La Paz
BOLIVIA
Sucre
CORDILLERA DE LOS ANDES
Antofagasta
PARAGUAY
Río de Janeiro
CHILE
Trópico de Capricornio
San Miguel
Asunción
de Tucumán
São Paulo
OCÉANO PACÍFICO
La Serena
Córdoba
Rosario
OCÉANO ATLÁNTICO
Valparaíso
URUGUAY
Santiago
ARGENTINA
Buenos Aires
Montevideo
Concepción
Río de la Plata
Bahía Blanca
Puerto Montt
Bariloche
Chiloé
AMÉRICA DEL SUR
Islas Malvinas
0   1500 kilómetros
Estrecho de Magallanes
Punta Arenas
Tierra del Fuego
0   1000 millas
Cabo de Hornos

MÉXICO, AMÉRICA CENTRAL Y EL CARIBE

San Diego
Mexicali • Phoenix
Tijuana
Tucson
Nogales
Ciudad Juárez
Chihuahua
Baja
California
Durango
La Paz
Monterrey
Mazatlán
Aguascalientes
MÉXICO
Santa Fe
Albuquerque
ESTADOS UNIDOS
El Paso
Dallas
San
Antonio
Austin
Houston
Nuevo
Laredo
Memphis
Atlanta
Nueva Orleans
San Agustín
Tampa
Miami
Nassau
**ISLAS
BAHAMAS**
**OCÉANO
ATLÁNTICO**
Golfo de México
Trópico de Cáncer
SIERRA MADRE OCCIDENTAL
SIERRA MADRE ORIENTAL
Golfo de California

Puerto Vallarta
Guadalajara
León
Manzanillo
Taxco
Guanajuato
Tampico
México, D.F.
Puebla
Veracruz
Acapulco
Oaxaca
SIERRA MADRE DEL SUR
*Bahía de
Campeche*
Mérida
Cozumel
Campeche
*Península
de
Yucatán*
La Habana
CUBA
Santiago de Cuba
JAMAICA
Kingston
Guantánamo
Santo
Domingo
HAITÍ
**PUERTO
RICO**
San Juan
**REPÚBLICA
DOMINICANA**
Puerto
Príncipe
MAR CARIBE
ANTILLAS MENORES
Caracas
Maracaibo
Mérida
VENEZUELA
Barranquilla
Cartagena
Medellín
Bogotá
Cali
COLOMBIA
BRASIL

Golfo de Tehuantepec
Guatemala
GUATEMALA
EL SALVADOR
San Salvador
BELICE
Belmopan
HONDURAS
Tegucigalpa
Managua
NICARAGUA
San José
COSTA RICA
*Golfo
de los
Mosquitos*
*Canal de
Panamá*
Panamá
PANAMÁ

**OCÉANO
PACÍFICO**

0 ___ 800 kilómetros
0 ___ 400 millas

ESPAÑA

MAR CANTÁBRICO
*Bahía de
Vizcaya*
FRANCIA
La Coruña
Santiago de
Compostela
GALICIA
Vigo
Oviedo
ASTURIAS
CANTABRIA
Santander
San Sebastián
Bilbao
**PAÍS
VASCO**
NAVARRA
Pamplona
LOS PIRINEOS
ANDORRA
*Golfo de
León*
León
CASTILLA-LEÓN
Burgos
Logroño
LA RIOJA
Zaragoza
CATALUÑA
Lérida
Costa Brava
Zamora
Valladolid
Río Duero
E S P A Ñ A
Río Ebro
Tarragona
Barcelona
Oporto
Salamanca
Segovia
SIERRA DE GUADARRAMA
ARAGÓN
Ávila
El Escorial
MADRID
Guadalajara
Madrid
Castellón
Menorca
Mallorca
**OCÉANO
ATLÁNTICO**
P O R T U G A L
Río Tajo
Cáceres
Toledo
**CASTILLA-
LA MANCHA**
Valencia
**COMUNIDAD
VALENCIANA**
Ibiza
Palma
ISLAS BALEARES
Lisboa
EXTREMADURA
Ciudad Real
Albacete
Alicante
Costa Blanca
Formentera
Badajoz
Mérida
Almadén
Murcia
MURCIA
Lorca
Cartagena
Río Guadiana
SIERRA MORENA
Linares
Río Guadalquivir
Córdoba
Jaén
Sevilla
ANDALUCÍA
SIERRA NEVADA
Granada
Almería
Huelva
Jerez de la Frontera
Málaga
*Golfo de
Cádiz*
Cádiz
Costa del Sol
Gibraltar (R.U.)
MAR MEDITERRÁNEO
Tánger
Ceuta (Esp.)
Orán

0 ___ 200 kilómetros
0 ___ 100 millas

ISLAS CANARIAS
Lanzarote
Santa Cruz
de Tenerife
Fuerte-
ventura
La
Palma
Tenerife
Las
Palmas
Hierro
Gomera
Las Palmas de Gran Canaria

ÁFRICA
Malabo
CAMERÚN
**GUINEA
ECUATORIAL**
GABÓN

Los espíritus[a]

Para pensar... [b]

In a moment you will watch the **Prólogo** to the movie *Sol y viento*. Examine the photos on this page. At this point, you may not see what they suggest about the plot and characters, but consider the following: characters often represent groups of people. What types of people are represented by each person you see in the photos? Can you imagine any kind of conflict that could develop among them?

[a]Los... *Spirits* [b]Para... *Something to think about . . .*

SOL Y VIENTO

Antes de ver[a] el episodio

[a]Antes... *Before watching*

You are about to watch the prologue of *Sol y viento*. In this brief episode, you will meet several principal characters, and a major plot line will be established. Before watching the episode, complete the activities in **Antes de ver el episodio.**

Actividad A

Consider the following questions.

1. What do the words **sol** and **viento** mean?
2. What roles to do you think the sun and the wind might play in a movie? What might they represent? Can you think of where words in the title suggest an underlying theme or presence in some other work of fiction (movie or novel)?

Actividad B Dos personajes (*characters*)

These are the two main characters you will meet in this episode. Try to determine which of the sentences for each character strikes you as true or likely based on a first impression from the photos.

▲ María Sánchez

1. Es profesora de economía.
2. Es española.
3. Es inteligente y dedicada.

▲ Jaime (James) Talavera

1. Es hombre de negocios (*businessman*).
2. Es español.
3. Es inteligente y sensible (*sensitive*).

Actividad C Un diálogo

In one scene, María speaks to her assistant. Read the dialogue and then select the word that you think best completes it.

> MARÍA: ¿Qué quieres,[a] Diego?
> DIEGO: Sólo quiero decirle[b] que
> _____ muy tarde.[c] Ya
> terminamos,[d] profesora.

[a]¿Qué... *What do you want* [b]Sólo... *I just want to tell you* [c]*late* [d]Ya... *We're finished*

a. es   **b.** tienes   **c.** hay

Actividad D El episodio

Now watch the episode. Don't worry if you don't understand everything in Spanish; just try to get the gist of what is going on.

Después de ver[e] el episodio

Actividad A ¿Qué recuerdas? (*What do you remember?*)

Answer each item based on what you remember from watching the **Prólogo**.

1. ¿Cómo se llama el señor que necesita viajar (*needs to travel*) a Chile?
   a. Andy   **b.** John   **c.** James
2. El señor está muy contento (*He is very happy*) con la idea de viajar (*traveling*) a Chile. ¿Cierto (*True*) o falso?
   a. cierto   **b.** falso
3. ¿Cuál es la relación entre María y Diego?
   a. Ella es estudiante y él es profesor.
   b. Él es estudiante y ella es profesora.
4. Probablemente, la especialización (*specialty*) de María es...
   a. matemáticas.   **b.** ingeniería.   **c.** antropología.

Actividad B ¿Lo captaste? (*Did you get it?*)

Go back to **Actividad C** of **Antes de ver el episodio** and verify your answer. Remember: If it helps, watch the corresponding section of the episode again.

Actividad C Utilizando (*Using*) el contexto

One skill you will want to develop as you study Spanish is guessing the meaning of language from context. Here are the first lines of the scene between María and Diego:

> DIEGO: Es lindo, ¿no?
> MARÍA: Sí. Es muy lindo.

[e]Después... *After watching* [f]Detrás de... *Behind*

Detrás de[f] la cámara

You probably noticed that one of the main characters is addressed in the **Prólogo** as "James," but his given name (and the name with which he grew up) is "Jaime." Why do you suppose he goes by James, the English equivalent of Jaime? What might this tell you about his character?

Keep this in mind as you watch future episodes of *Sol y viento*. In what other ways may Jaime/James have left his past behind?

Go back and watch this scene again without looking up any words. What are they talking about and what do you think **lindo** means?

Actividad D Intercambio (*Exchange*)

You can use the following adjectives with the verb **ser** to describe some of the characters you have seen in the **Prólogo.** What statements can you make about María, James, Andy, or the **machi?** Share your statements with the class.

1. bilingüe
2. chileno/a (*Chilean*)
3. sabio/a (*wise*)
4. persistente
5. guapo/a (*good-looking*)

▲ María   ▲ Jaime (James)   ▲ Andy   ▲ la machi

Note

You have just completed viewing the **Prólogo** of *Sol y viento* and have worked through the activities in this section. Note that, from here on in, you will view the episodes at least twice. The activities contained in each section are structured in a way to help you do this. Enjoy watching *Sol y viento!*

La llegada^a

Para pensar...

In the first photo, where is Jaime, and who is the man speaking with him? Could he have something to do with the Sol y viento winery?

In the second photo, Jaime is talking on the phone to someone. Where do you think he is? Who is he talking to? And who is the man sitting at the desk in the third photo? What do you think his mood is? Does he look happy? Worried?

SOL Y VIENTO

A primera vista

Antes de ver el episodio

Actividad A ¿Qué recuerdas?

Think briefly about what you know regarding the movie *Sol y viento* thus far. Which of the following are true?

1. ☐ Jaime desea ir (*to go*) a Chile.
2. ☐ Jaime habla inglés y español.
3. ☐ Jaime trabaja para una compañía norteamericana.
4. ☐ María es antropóloga y profesora.
5. ☐ La machi habla de un conflicto.

Actividad B   Vocabulario útil (*useful*)

Paso 1 Look over the following words and phrases. You will need them in **Paso 2**.

a propósito	by the way
¡claro que sí!	of course!
para servirlo	at your service
¿qué se le ofrece?	how can I help you?

Paso 2 Using the words and phrases from **Paso 1**, complete the following exchange between a clerk (**empleado**) and a customer (**cliente**).

CLIENTE: Disculpe.[a]
EMPLEADO: _____,[1] señor. _____.[2]
CLIENTE: Busco una camisa de seda.[b] ¿Tienen Uds.?[c]
EMPLEADO: _____.[3] Pase Ud. por aquí, por favor.
CLIENTE: _____:[4] Sólo[d] tengo cheques de viajero.[e] ¿Es problema?
EMPLEADO: No, señor. ¿Tiene Ud. pasaporte?
CLIENTE: Cómo no.[f]

[a]*Excuse me.* [b]*camisa... silk shirt* [c]*¿Tienen... Do you have any?* [d]*Only* [e]*cheques... traveler's checks* [f]*Cómo... Of course.*

Actividad C   ¿Qué falta (*is missing*)?

Paso 1 Here is part of the exchange between Mario and Jaime in the hotel lobby that you haven't yet seen or read. Select from the choices below to fill in each blank.

MARIO: _____¹ diez mil
pesos, señor.
JAIME: Aquí tiene. _____.²
(*Mario turns and
walks away. Jaime
calls to him.*) ¡Oiga!
¡Espere!
MARIO: ¿Sí, señor? Diga,
nomás.ᵃ
JAIME: ¿Ud. hace viajes
fuera deᵇ Santiago?

ᵃDiga... *Just say the word.* ᵇ¿Ud.... *Do you take trips outside*

1. **a.** Es
   b. Hay
   c. Son
   d. Están

2. **a.** Por favor (*Please*)
   b. Gracias (*Thank you*)
   c. De nada (*You're welcome*)

As you may recall from the **Prólogo** of *Sol y viento*, Jaime was not too happy about having to go to Chile. He believes that his bilingualism and knowledge of wines were the company's motivating factors for sending him. What is Jaime's background? In a future episode you will hear Jaime talk about himself, but here is some relevant information. He grew up in the Central Valley of California, where his parents and grandparents were farm workers who harvested grapes for the many vineyards in that state. Intelligent and motivated, like many upwardly mobile first-generation children of immigrants, he attended college and graduate school, eventually winding up in the corporate world and leaving his roots and past behind. Or has he?

Paso 2 Look at the exchange one more time. What do you think Jaime is saying when Mario turns and walks away?

Actividad D   El episodio

Now watch the episode. Remember that it's OK to let some words and expressions slip by you, especially since this is the first time you are watching the episode. You should be able to follow along without understanding every single word. You will watch the episode again in **A segunda vista** (*Upon a second viewing*), and you will understand more then.

Después de ver el episodio

Actividad A   ¿Qué recuerdas?

Answer each item according to what you remember from the episode.

1. Cuando Jaime llega a su habitación (*room*), está cansado (*tired*). ¿Sí o no?
2. ¿Cómo se llama el hotel donde se queda (*is staying*) Jaime?
3. Mañana Jaime necesita ir al Valle del _____.
4. ¿Cuál es el apellido de Jaime? ¿Y el de Mario?
5. En su habitación, Jaime habla por teléfono con...
   a. Andy, de Bartel Aquapower **b.** Carlos Sánchez, de «Sol y viento»
6. ¿Qué palabra describe mejor (*best*) la expresión de Carlos al final?
   a. preocupación (*worry*)   **b.** alegría (*happiness*)
   c. indiferencia

Actividad B   ¿Lo captaste?

Go back to **Actividad C** of **Antes de ver el episodio** to verify your answers. If you need to, watch that particular section of the episode again.

Actividad C Utilizando el contexto

Paso 1 You have already begun to learn the skill of guessing the meaning of language in context. Did you deduce the meanings of the following phrases in italics? Watch this scene in the episode again if it helps.

> JAIME: Al Hotel Bonaparte. *¿A cuánto sale?*
> MARIO: Eh, um, unos 10.000 (diez mil) pesos, más o menos. *¿Le parece bien?*
> JAIME: Sí. Vamos.

Paso 2 Another skill you have begun to work on is noting that a word or phrase can have multiple meanings. For example, Jaime says **Sí. Vamos.** in response to Mario. **Vamos** means *we go* or *we are going,* but does that make sense in this context? What do you think is the equivalent of **vamos** in this context?

Actividad D En resumen (*In summary*)

Paso 1 You have now been introduced to Jaime and Mario. How would you describe their personalities, based on your initial impressions? In what ways are they similar, if at all? In what ways are they different? Use adjectives you know to describe each in several sentences.

Nota sobre el lenguaje

One way to express future intent is with the verb **ir** (*to go*) plus the preposition **a** and an infinitive, as in **Voy a ver una película esta noche** (*I'm going to see a movie tonight*). Note, however, that the forms of **ir** are irregular.

voy	**vamos**
vas	**vais**
va	**van**

You will learn more about the uses of **ir** throughout your study of Spanish.

A segunda vista

Antes de ver el episodio

Actividad A ¡A escuchar! (*Let's listen!*)

In a moment you will watch **Episodio 1** once again. But first, familiarize yourself with the following excerpt from the episode in which Jaime calls Carlos at the winery. You will be asked to listen closely and write the missing words in the blanks. Do not look back at any previous excerpts from this episode!

> JAIME: ¿Aló, _____^{1} «Sol y viento»?... Don Carlos Sánchez... Ah, _____^{2} él. Bien. _____^{3} Jaime Talavera, de los Estados Unidos. Compañía Bartel Aquapower... Sí, claro _____^{4} hablo español. Ya _____^{5} aquí... No, en Santiago. Mañana voy a verlo, _____^{6} a mediodía.
>
> CARLOS: _____,^{7} señor Talavera. Lo _____^{8} mañana. _____^{9} entonces. Chau.

Actividad B El episodio

Now watch the episode again. Remember to pay close attention to the scene in which Jaime calls Carlos on the phone and to write down the missing words for **Actividad A.**

Después de ver el episodio

Actividad Intercambio

Consider the following questions in English. In later chapters you'll be able to offer such opinions in Spanish.

1. How would you describe Carlos' expression at the end of the episode?
2. Why does he have this expression?

Hint: Keep in mind the boardroom scene from the **Prólogo** when the three men discuss the situation in Chile.

If you need to, watch this scene again and see if you can determine anything by the way Carlos talks as well.

SOL Y VIENTO: Enfoque cultural

In **Episodio 1** of *Sol y viento*, Jaime arrives at the airport in Santiago, where he is greeted by an enthusiastic driver, Mario. Santiago, like any major city in the Spanish-speaking world, offers both private drivers like Mario as well as regular public taxis. However, taxi systems and taxi drivers vary from city to city. In Santiago, they are safe, clean, and convenient, and as in any great city there are lots of them. As in this country, in Chile the fare is calculated by meters, and there is no need to negotiate a price (unless you use a private taxi). In Mexico City, in contrast, you generally have to ask how much it will cost to get to your destination before getting in the taxi. If not, you may wind up paying much more than you should, as those taxis may not use meters. Nonetheless, in most Spanish-speaking countries outside of Spain, taxi rides tend to be less expensive than they are in this country.

▲ Hay muchos taxis en México, D.F.*

Para escribir

Antes de escribir

For this activity, you will compare and contrast Jaime and Mario. From the following list of adjectives, decide which ones best describe either character (or both).

ADJETIVOS	JAIME	MARIO
1. guapo (*handsome*)	☐	☐
2. ambicioso	☐	☐
3. simpático (*nice*)	☐	☐
4. joven (*young*)	☐	☐
5. inteligente	☐	☐
6. trabajador (*hard-working*)	☐	☐

*D.F. = **Distrito Federal,** much like Washington, D.C. (District of Columbia)

ADJETIVOS	JAIME	MARIO
7. bilingüe	☐	☐
8. serio	☐	☐
9. gregario	☐	☐
10. reservado	☐	☐

A escribir

Paso 1 Now that you have made some preliminary decisions about the personalities of these two characters, you must decide how you will organize your thoughts. Select one of the following possibilities:

☐ write about Jaime first, then Mario

☐ write about Mario first, then Jaime

☐ use the personality traits to compare and contrast each person as you go

Paso 2 Now draft your description on a separate sheet of paper. The following phrases may be helpful in writing out your descriptions.

al contrario	on the other hand
en cambio	on the other hand
igualmente	equally
no tanto	not as much
pero	but
sin embargo	however
también	also
y	and

El encuentro[a]

Para pensar...

In the first photo on this page, Jaime Talavera meets a young woman. Do you think she will have anything to do with Jaime's work in Chile? Or will she have a role in his personal life? Could it have something to do with the piece of paper that Jaime is reading?

In the third photo, we see Mario and Jaime smiling. What do you think they're smiling about? Could it be related to the title of this episode?

[a]*encounter*

SOL Y VIENTO

A primera vista

Antes de ver el episodio

Actividad A   ¿Qué recuerdas?

Indicate whether the following statements are **cierto** or **falso,** based on what you've seen so far in *Sol y viento.*

	CIERTO	FALSO
1. Jaime tiene ganas de ir a Santiago.	☐	☐
2. Jaime ya sabe (*already knows*) mucho de vinos.	☐	☐
3. Mario no puede llevar a Jaime al Valle del Maipo.	☐	☐
4. El hotel donde Jaime se aloja (*is staying*) se llama Hotel Bonaparte.	☐	☐
5. Jaime necesita hablar con Andrés Sánchez de la viña «Sol y viento».	☐	☐

Actividad B   Vocabulario útil

Paso 1   Look over the words and phrases that follow. You will need them in **Paso 2.**

¡espere!	wait!
ojalá que nos veamos de nuevo	I hope we see each other again
¡qué coincidencia!	what a coincidence!

Paso 2   Using the words and phrases from **Paso 1,** complete the following exchange between a man and a woman who have just met.

HOMBRE: Soy Juan Molino y trabajo en la universidad.

MUJER: _____[1] ¡Yo también! Yo trabajo en el departamento de química. ¿En qué departamento trabaja Ud.?

HOMBRE: Soy profesor de biología. ¡Somos vecinos![a] _____.[2]

MUJER: Igualmente. Bueno, Juan Molino, tengo que irme.[b]

HOMBRE: _____[3] No sé[c] cómo se llama Ud.

MUJER: ¡Ah, perdón! Soy Alicia Rodríguez.

[a]*neighbors*   [b]*tengo... I have to leave*   [c]*No... I don't know*

Actividad C ¿Qué falta?

Here is part of the exchange that you have not yet seen between Jaime, María, and Mario in front of the hotel. Select from the choices to fill in each blank.

MARIO: Buenos días, don Jaime...
¡Lo esperaba!ª

JAIME: Fuiᵇ a _____¹ un poco.
Bueno, hasta aquí llego yo.
¿_____² que la llevemosᶜ a algún sitio?

MARIA: No, gracias. Mi trabajo _____³ cerca de aquí. Puedo
_____.⁴

ªLo... *I was waiting for you!* ᵇ*I went* ᶜ*que... us to take you*

1. **a.** charlar   **b.** correr   **c.** levantar pesas (*lift weights*)
2. **a.** Quiere   **b.** Tiene   **c.** Puede
3. **a.** es   **b.** no es   **c.** está
4. **a.** caminar (*walk*)   **b.** hablar   **c.** bailar

Actividad D El episodio

Now watch the episode. Don't worry if there are things you don't understand. You should be able to follow most of what happens without understanding every single word. You will watch the episode again in **A segunda vista,** and you will understand more then.

Después de ver el episodio

Actividad A ¿Qué recuerdas?

Answer each question according to what you remember from the episode.

1. ¿Qué ejercicio hace Jaime en el parque?
   a. Juega al fútbol (*soccer*).   **b.** Corre.   **c.** Hace ejercicios aeróbicos.

2. ¿Cuánto cuesta el papelito de la suerte (*fortune*)?

    a. tres pesos   **b.** trece pesos   **c.** trescientos (300) pesos

3. ¿Cómo sabe Jaime el nombre de María? Lo sabe por (*because of*)...

    a. el papelito de la suerte.   **b.** los libros de ella.   **c.** su tarjeta (*card*).

4. María trabaja en dos lugares: en la universidad y en...

    a. el Hotel Bonaparte.   **b.** un sitio de excavación.   **c.** el Parque Forestal.

5. El papelito dice que _____ es un torbellino (*whirlwind*).

    a. el amor   **b.** la antropóloga   **c.** el tiempo

6. Al final del episodio, ¿quién parece (*seems*) tener más interés en el papelito de la suerte?

    a. Jaime   **b.** Mario

Actividad B   ¿Lo captaste?

Go back to **Actividad C** of **Antes de ver el episodio** to verify your answers. If you need to, watch that particular section of the episode again.

Actividad C   Utilizando el contexto

You have already begun to learn the skill of guessing the meaning of language in context. Did you deduce the meanings of the following phrases in italics? Watch this scene between Jaime, the kid (**el cabrito**), and María again if you think it will help.

    JAIME: ¡Le pido mil disculpas! *Andaba distraído.*
    CABRITO: El señor *estaba leyendo* el papelito de la suerte.
    MARÍA: Ah. Debe ser una suerte excepcional.

Actividad D   En resumen

Complete the description of the episode you have just watched by inserting the words and phrases on the right into the appropriate spaces.

En este episodio, Jaime _____[1] en el Parque Forestal. Ve a[a] un hombre que _____[2] papelitos de la suerte. Jaime _____[3] el papelito y de repente[b] _____[4] una mujer. Es María Sánchez. Jaime le pide disculpas[c] y María sigue caminando.[d] Jaime _____[5] caminar con María hasta el Hotel Bonaparte donde Mario lo _____.[6] Los tres _____[7] un rato[e] y luego María _____[8] irse.

corre
decide
espera (*waits*)
hablan
lee
necesita
se choca con (*he bumps into*)
vende

[a]Ve... *He sees*   [b]de... *suddenly*   [c]le... *apologizes*   [d]sigue... *keeps walking*
[e]un... *a while*

16

A segunda vista

Antes de ver el episodio

Actividad A ¡A escuchar!

In a moment you will watch **Episodio 2** once again. Familiarize yourself with the following excerpt from the scene in which Jaime talks with a young boy (**cabrito**) in the park. You will be asked to listen closely and write the missing words in the blank. Do not look back at any previous excerpts from this episode!

JAIME: ¿_____¹ pesos?
CABRITO: ¡Chis! ¡_____² pesos no, señor! ¡Son _____³ pesos!
JAIME: Ah, espere.
CABRITO: _____,⁴ _____⁵ y _____.⁶ Ya, _____.⁷
JAIME: Ah, y _____⁸ cien son para ti.
CABRITO: ¡Gracias, señor!

Actividad B El episodio

Now watch the episode again. Remember to pay close attention to the scene in which Jaime talks to the young boy in the park and to write down the missing words for **Actividad A.**

Después de ver el episodio

Actividad Intercambio

In this episode Jaime reads that love is a whirlwind (**El amor es un torbellino.**). With which of the following statements about love would you agree?

El amor es...

a. un túnel sin salida (*without an exit*).

b. ciego (*blind*).

c. un dolor (*ache, pain*) que no se puede curar.

d. como un accidente. No sabes cuándo va a ocurrir.

Detrás de la cámara

If you watch María carefully, you may have noticed that she has a determined walk. Even when she's in the park, she never strolls leisurely. What might that say about her personality? María is very goal-oriented, and she doesn't stop until she achieves her goals. Jaime seems to pick up on this, and perhaps that is why he is so persistent. Jaime realizes intuitively that María possesses much more than good looks. That's why when Mario says "¡Bonita la muchacha, don Jaime!" Jaime emphasizes that she's also intelligent. Do you think Jaime and María would make a good match? Are they too much alike? Too dissimilar? Or is the combination just right?

SOL Y VIENTO: Enfoque cultural

City parks abound in Spanish-speaking countries, as they do in this country. However, they are often used in different ways. In **Episodio 2** you watched Jaime as he jogged through the Parque Forestal in Santiago. However, using a public park as a place to exercise is not the norm for most Spanish-speaking people. Instead, parks are often places to socialize, and on Sundays they may flourish with couples and families of all ages out for an old-fashioned Sunday afternoon stroll (**el paseo**). It is also typical to find vendors of all types in these parks selling everything from cotton candy to balloons, as well as entertainers working for donations, such as the organ-grinding fortune teller with his parrot that you will see in this episode. Some well-known parks in Spanish-speaking cities include the Retiro (Madrid), Lazema (Buenos Aires), and Chapultepec (Mexico City), among others.

▲ El parque Chapultepec (México, D.F.)

Para escribir

Antes de escribir

For this activity, you will describe your first impressions of María and decide if she and Jaime have similar personalities. First, choose the adjectives from the following list that best describe María, according to your first impressions.

Creo que María es...

☐ aburrida   ☐ enérgica
☐ alegre   ☐ ingenua (*naive*)
☐ ambiciosa   ☐ inteligente
☐ bonita (*pretty*)   ☐ introvertida
☐ desconfiada (*untrusting*) ☐ reservada
☐ divertida   ☐ seria

A escribir

Paso 1 Now that you have made some preliminary decisions about your first impressions of María, decide how you will organize your thoughts. Select one of the following possibilities:

☐ describe each character and then write about how María and Jaime are more similar than different

☐ describe each character and then write about how María and Jaime are more different than similar

Paso 2 Now draft your composition on a separate sheet of paper. The following phrases may be helpful in writing out your descriptions. You should also review the phrases from the **Para escribir** section of **Episodio 1.**

además	furthermore, in addition
creo que...	I think that . . .
me parece que...	it seems to me that . . .
(no) son (muy) parecidos	they're (not) (very) similar

A la viña[a]

Para pensar...

Jaime y Mario llegan a la viña «Sol y viento». En una de las fotos, Jaime habla con un hombre. ¿Quién es el hombre? ¿De qué van a hablar?

En otra foto ese hombre ofrece un brindis.[b] ¿Por qué o por quién brinda?

[a]A... *To the winery* [b]ofrece... *offers a toast* **21**

SOL Y VIENTO

A primera vista

Antes de ver el episodio

Actividad A ¿Qué recuerdas?

Indica si las siguientes oraciones son ciertas o falsas según (*according to*) lo que recuerdas del **Episodio 2** de *Sol y viento*.

	CIERTO	FALSO
1. Jaime juega al frisbee en un parque de Santiago.	☐	☐
2. Jaime se choca con María mientras lee un papelito de la suerte.	☐	☐
3. María trabaja en una excavación en el Valle del Maipo.	☐	☐
4. María permite que Jaime se quede con (*keep*) su tarjeta.	☐	☐
5. A Jaime no le importa (*Jaime doesn't care about*) la inteligencia de María.	☐	☐

Actividad B Vocabulario útil

Paso 1 Estudia las siguientes palabras y frases.

la bodega	wine cellar
la botella	bottle
la copa de vino	glass of wine
la cosecha	harvest
el merlot (un vino tinto)	merlot (a red wine)
el tonel	barrel
¡salud!	cheers!
se dejará de producir	it will stop being produced

Paso 2 Empareja (*Match*) cada una de las definiciones con la palabra correspondiente del **Paso 1**.

1. ____ El vino se vende (*is sold*) en este recipiente (*container*).
2. ____ El vino se sirve (*is served*) en esto.
3. ____ Es una habitación (*room*) grande donde se almacenan (*are stored*) los vinos.
4. ____ Es un recipiente de madera (*wood*) donde se añeja (*is aged*) el vino.
5. ____ Son las uvas (*grapes*) después de ser recogidas (*picked*) de las viñas (*vines*).
6. ____ Es un vino tinto.

a. la copa
b. el merlot
c. la cosecha
d. la bodega
e. el tonel
f. la botella

Actividad C ¿Qué falta?

En el **Episodio 3** de *Sol y viento* vas a ver una escena en que Carlos y Jaime toman una copa de vino mientras hablan. A continuación (*Following*) hay unos fragmentos de su diálogo.

> CARLOS: ¡Salud!
> JAIME: Hmmm... Delicioso... y un
> _____[1] color. Un
> merlot, si no me equivoco.[a]
> CARLOS: Correcto. Una cosecha muy especial, del 88. ¿Ud. _____[2]
> algo de vinos?
> JAIME: Sí, algo. _____[3] pronto se dejará de producir.

[a]si... *if I'm not mistaken*

Indica la respuesta más adecuada para cada espacio en blanco.

1. **a.** tan claro   **b.** excelente   **c.** monótono (*drab*)
2. **a.** dice   **b.** lee   **c.** sabe
3. **a.** Qué bueno que (*Good thing that*)   **c.** Es cierto que (*It's certain that*)
   b. Lástima que (*Too bad that*)

Actividad D El episodio

Ahora mira el episodio. Si hay algo que no entiendes bien, puedes volver a ver la escena en cuestión.

Después de ver el episodio

Actividad A ¿Qué recuerdas?

Contesta cada pregunta basándote en lo que recuerdas del **Episodio 3**.

1. ¿Quién es Traimaqueo?
   a. un miembro de la familia Sánchez   **b.** un trabajador de la viña
2. Don Carlos está nervioso al reunirse con (*upon meeting*) Jaime. ¿Cierto o falso?
   a. cierto   **b.** falso
3. Carlos le dice a Jaime que su madre y su hermana están...
   a. en Santiago.   **b.** en casa.
4. Según Carlos, su hermana no tiene interés en los asuntos (*matters*) de la viña. ¿Cierto o falso?
   a. cierto   **b.** falso
5. Don Carlos y sus trabajadores están planeando...
   a. una recepción para celebrar un vino nuevo.
   b. una fiesta de cumpleaños (*birthday party*).
6. Jaime le dice a don Carlos que la venta (*sale*) tiene que suceder (*happen*) en los próximos días. ¿Cierto o falso?
   a. cierto   **b.** falso

After his father's death, Carlos assumed sole responsibility for managing the family winery, perhaps at an age when he was not yet ready or willing to do so. Lacking his father's good guidance, Carlos developed a stern and relentless demeanor that is immediately evident in the way he talks down to his workers. In short, Carlos orders people around because he can. The other members of the Sánchez family do not inquire into the runnings of the winery and as a result, his authority is unquestioned.

Actividad B ¿Lo captaste?

Vuelve a (*Return to*) la **Actividad C** en **Antes de ver el episodio** para verificar tus respuestas. Si es necesario, vuelve a ver el episodio.

Actividad C Utilizando el contexto

Ya sabes que es difícil interpretar pronombres directos sin contexto. Al ver (*Upon watching*) más episodios de *Sol y viento*, trata de usar tus conocimientos (*knowledge*) del trama (*plot*) para ayudarte a identificar los pronombres. Considera el diálogo a continuación.

> JAIME: ¿Le molesta si primero doy[a] un tour por la viña?
> CARLOS: No, para nada. Pero yo necesito quedarme aquí en la oficina. Traimaqueo lo puede guiar. Yo lo voy a llamar a su celular. ¿Sabe llegar?

[a] *I take*

Basándote en el contexto, ¿a quién se refiere **lo** en **Traimaqueo lo puede guiar**? ¿Y en **Yo lo voy a llamar a su celular**?

Actividad D En resumen

Completa la narración con las palabras y expresiones apropiadas de la lista.

En este episodio, Jaime visita la viña «Sol y viento», donde _____[1] a don Carlos, el administrador de la viña. Carlos y Jaime _____[2] una copa de vino en la oficina de Carlos mientras[a] _____[3] de finalizar la _____[4] de la viña. Jaime _____[5] finalizarlo todo dentro de[b] pocos días. Sin embargo,[c] Carlos no _____[6] las firmas[d] necesarias, y por eso Jaime _____[7] en no irse del Valle del Maipo sin un _____[8] firmado.[e]

conoce (*he meets*)
contrato
insiste
hablan
quiere
tiene
toman
venta

[a] *while* [b] *dentro... within* [c] *Sin... Nevertheless* [d] *signatures* [e] *signed*

A segunda vista

Antes de ver el episodio

Actividad A ¡A escuchar!

Pronto vas a volver a ver el **Episodio 3.**
Repasa brevemente el siguiente fragmento
del diálogo entre Carlos y Jaime. Cuando
veas el episodio, llena los espacios en
blanco con las palabras correctas. ¡No vuelvas a ver otros fragmentos de este episodio!

JAIME: Bonita _____.[1]
CARLOS: Y muy buen _____.[2]
¿Quisiera[a] hacer un breve recorrido?[b] ¿Le gusta el _____[3]?
JAIME: Sí, me gusta mucho, pero _____[4] esperar. Tenemos
negocios[c] _____.[5] ¿No es cierto?
CARLOS: Bueno, sí. Es cierto. ¿Por qué no vamos a mi _____[6]
para tener así más privacidad?

[a]*Would you like* [b]*tour* [c]*business*

Actividad B El episodio

Ahora mira el episodio de nuevo. No te olvides de (*Don't forget*) prestar
atención a la escena en que Carlos y Jaime se conocen (*meet each
other*) y apunta (*jot down*) las palabras que faltan para la **Actividad
A.** Puedes mirar el episodio más de una vez si quieres.

Después de ver el episodio

Actividad Intercambio

Paso 1 Piensa en tu
opiniones sobre las si-
guientes preguntas. Si es
necesario, vuelve a ver la
escena en cuestión.

1. ¿Cómo
describirías
(*would you
describe*) la
interacción entre
Carlos y
Traimaqueo cuando llega Jaime a la viña?
2. ¿Tienes una buena o mala relación? ¿Qué evidencia tienes
para apoyar (*support*) tu opinión?

SOL Y VIENTO: Enfoque cultural

En el **Episodio 3**, Jaime y Mario llegan al Valle del Maipo, y Mario compra unas empanadas para Jaime y para él. En muchos países hispanos, sobre todo en Latinoamérica, son típicos estos puestos[a] pequeños donde se vende comida. En Puerto Rico, al lado de algunas carreteras[b] hay puestos con letreros hechos a mano[c] que anuncian «pollo asado y frutas». En México, es típico ver en la ciudad puestos pequeños en forma de «carritos»[d] donde se venden tacos y tortas (sándwiches). En las zonas rurales, son más comunes los lugares pequeños como el puesto en donde Mario compró[e] las empanadas. Este tipo de comida tiene mucha demanda: es barata y se encuentra por todas partes en los países latinos. Pero, lo principal[f] es que les ofrece a personas de pocos recursos[g] la oportunidad de ganar algún dinero.

▲ Unos puestos de comida en México.

[a]*stands* [b]*highways* [c]*letreros... hand-made signs* [d]*carts* [e]*bought* [f]*lo... the main thing* [g]*financial resources*

Para escribir

Antes de escribir

Para esta actividad, vas a escribir una breve composición sobre los gustos (*likes*) de Jaime y de Carlos. Para comenzar, indica si las afirmaciones (*statements*) se refieren a Jaime, a Carlos o a los dos (**ambos**), según lo que crees.

	JAIME	CARLOS	AMBOS
1. Le gusta darse aires (*to put on airs*).	☐	☐	☐
2. Le gusta su trabajo.	☐	☐	☐
3. Le gusta mandar (*to give orders*).	☐	☐	☐
4. No le gusta esperar.	☐	☐	☐
5. Le gusta ir al grano (*to get to the point*).	☐	☐	☐
6. Le gustan los vinos chilenos.	☐	☐	☐
7. Le gustan los negocios.	☐	☐	☐
8. No le gustan las sorpresas (*surprises*).	☐	☐	☐

A escribir

Paso 1 Ahora que tienes algunas ideas sobre los gustos de cada personaje, ¿cómo vas a organizarlas? Escoge (*Choose*) una de las posibilidades a continuación:

☐ escribir sobre los gustos de Jaime primero, y luego sobre los de (*those of*) Carlos

☐ escribir sobre los gustos de Carlos, y luego sobre los de Jaime

☐ comparar a los dos simultáneamente, según la lista de afirmaciones en el **Paso 1**

Paso 2 Ahora redacta (*draft*) tu composición en una hoja de papel aparte (*separate sheet of paper*). Las siguientes palabras y frases te pueden ser útiles al redactar tu composición.

por otro lado	on the other hand
por un lado	on the one hand
también	also
tampoco	either; neither

Otro encuentro

Para pensar...

Basándote en las fotos, ¿a qué encuentro(s) se refiere el título de este episodio? ¿Quién es el señor que habla con Jaime? ¿De qué están hablando ellos? Y la figura en la mano[a] de Jaime, ¿qué representa? ¿Crees que María está contenta de ver a Jaime de nuevo?

[a]hand

SOL Y VIENTO

A primera vista

Antes de ver el episodio

Actividad A ¿Qué recuerdas?

¿Qué recuerdas hasta el momento? Escribe el nombre de los personajes apropiados en los espacios. Pero antes de empezar, lee la breve **Nota sobre el lenguaje** que aparece a continuación.

1. Después de correr, _____ compró una fortuna.
2. Al leer (*Upon reading*) su fortuna, se chocó con (*he bumped into*) _____, una profesora de antropología.
3. _____ lo llevó a la viña «Sol y viento». Allí habló con _____ sobre la venta de la viña.
4. No pudo ver a _____. _____ le dijo a Jaime que ella se fue a Santiago.

Nota sobre el lenguaje

If you haven't yet learned the formation of the preterite, one of the past tenses in Spanish, here is a quick guide for talking about someone else's activities in the past:

-**ar** verbs end in **-ó**: **habló** (*he/she spoke*), **caminó** (*he/she walked*)

-**er/-ir** verbs end in **-ió**: **corrió** (*he/she ran*), **salió** (*he/she went out / left*)

Some frequently used verbs do not follow this pattern, such as **dijo (decir)**, **pudo (poder)**, **estuvo (estar)**, and **fue (ir)**. You will learn more about past tenses throughout your study of Spanish.

Actividad B Vocabulario útil

Paso 1 Estudia las siguientes palabras y frases.

las cepas	vinestocks
los dioses	gods
me enterrarán	they will bury me (I will be buried)
nací	I was born
los pies	feet
púrpura	purple
el regalo	gift
la sangre	blood
se equivocan	(they) fool themselves
el topacio	topaz

Paso 2 Usa las palabras y frases del **Paso 1** para completar cada oración a continuación. **¡OJO!** No se usan todas las palabras y frases.

1. Según algunos, el vino es un _____ de los dioses, algo especial.

2. Para hacer buen vino, son importantes el sol, la tierra y claro, las _____.

3. Soy muy orgulloso (*proud*) de mi lugar de origen. _____ aquí y _____ aquí.

4. Muchas personas _____ porque creen que el dinero hace su vida mejor, pero no siempre es así.

5. El _____ es una piedra (*stone*) preciosa que puede ser de varios colores.

Actividad C ¿Qué falta?

En este episodio, Jaime oye a Traimaqueo decir que doña Isabel lo espera en la casa. Lee el diálogo entre Jaime y Traimaqueo.

YOLANDA: Oye, viejo.* ¿Vas a llegar muy tarde?

TRAIMAQUEO: Un poquito. La señora Isabel me espera en la casa.

JAIME: Creía que la señora Isabel estaba† en Santiago.

TRAIMAQUEO: No, no, no. La señora Isabel no hace muchos viajes en estos días. _____.

¿Qué razón crees que va a ofrecer Traimaqueo para explicar por qué doña Isabel no hace muchos viajes?

a. La señora está muy ocupada (*busy*) con la viña.

b. La señora no está de muy buena salud (*health*).

Actividad D El episodio

Ahora mira el episodio. Si hay algo que no entiendes bien, puedes volver a ver la escena en cuestión.

Después de ver el episodio

Actividad A ¿Qué recuerdas?

Contesta cada pregunta sobre el **Episodio 4**.

1. ¿Quién le dio un tour de la viña a Jaime? ¿Los acompañó Mario?

2. Cuando Jaime oyó que doña Isabel estaba en casa, decidió ir a verla en seguida. ¿Sí o no?

3. ¿Le dijo Carlos la verdad a Jaime? ¿Sí o no?

4. ¿Para quién compró Jaime la figurita del espíritu mapuche?

---

*Viejo/a is a term of endearment often used among people who have known each other for a long time. It is used more typically among married people.
†Estaba is a past-tense verb form, called the *imperfect*, that you will learn about in the next **episodio.** In this context, it means (*she*) *was.*

Actividad B ¿Lo captaste?

Ahora verifica tu respuesta a la **Actividad C** de **Antes de ver el episodio.** Puedes ver esa escena de nuevo si quieres.

Actividad C Utilizando el contexto

¿Pudiste deducir el significado de las palabras y expresiones que aparecen *en letra cursiva*, según el contexto en que aparecen?

1.   TRAIMAQUEO: Pasemos a la viña, *¿le parece?*
2.   JAIME: ¿Tiene algún significado esta figurita?
       ... *¿A cuánto me sale?*
       TENDERA (*Shopkeeper*): Diecinueve mil quinientos pesos.
       JAIME: Perfecto. *Me la llevo.*

Actividad D En resumen

Completa la siguiente narración con las palabras y expresiones apropiadas de la lista a la derecha.

En este episodio, Jaime _____[1] la viña «Sol y viento» gracias a un tour que le da Traimaqueo. Al final del tour, Traimaqueo recita parte de un _____[2] sobre el vino, demostrando[a] su _____[3] por el vino. Jaime llega a saber que Carlos no es una persona honesta, pues le mintió[b] sobre su _____[4] Más tarde, Jaime tiene un encuentro _____[5] con María. Ella está en el mercado colocando[c] anuncios en apoyo[d] del _____.[6] Jaime le da una sorpresa: una figurita del _____[7] protector de los mapuches. ¿Cómo crees que van las relaciones entre Jaime y María?

agradable
conoce
espíritu (*m.*)
madre
pasión (*f.*)
poema (*m.*)
pueblo mapuche

[a]*showing* [b]*he lied* [c]*hanging* [d]*support*

A segunda vista

Antes de ver el episodio

Actividad A ¡A escuchar!

Vas a ver el **Episodio 4** de nuevo. Primero, repasa la siguiente escena. Luego, mientras la veas, completa lo que dicen los personajes con las palabras y expresiones que oyes.

MARÍA: Bueno, además de ser _____,[1] trabajo por los derechos[a] del pueblo mapuche.

JAIME: ¡Ah! Entonces, a lo mejor le gusta esto. Es _____[2] Ud.

MARÍA: ¿Para míííí? ¡Oye! ¡Qué _____![3] ¿Cómo sabía... ?

JAIME: Su _____.[4]

MARÍA: ¡Ah, por supuesto![b]

[a]*rights* [b]*por... of course*

Actividad B El episodio

Ahora mira el episodio de nuevo. No te olvides de hacer la **Actividad A** en **Antes de ver el episodio** mientras lo ves. Puedes mirar el episodio más de una vez si quieres.

Después de ver el episodio

Actividad Intercambio

Ya sabes que Carlos le mintió a Jaime en cuanto a la ausencia de la señora Isabel. Contesta las siguientes preguntas.

1. ¿Por qué mintió Carlos? ¿Esconde algo?
2. ¿Hay algún problema en la viña? ¿Cuál es?
3. ¿Qué sabe doña Isabel de la venta de «Sol y viento»?

SOL Y VIENTO: Enfoque cultural

En el **Episodio 4,** María coloca carte-les[a] para una reunión a favor de los mapuches. Como muchas personas en Latinoamérica, María lucha[b] por los dere-chos de los grupos indígenas que no tienen voz[c] ni mucha influencia en la política de su país. El activismo por los indígenas no se limita a Chile sino también se observa en México, el Paraguay, Guatemala, el Perú y otros países. Muchas veces estos indígenas no tienen suficiente conocimiento del idioma español, lo cual impide su partici-pación activa en la sociedad. En tales[d] casos necesitan de personas como María que los ayudan a obtener los beneficios que les co-rresponden según las leyes[e] del país.

▲ Un indígena ecuatoriano

Además, luchan por un sistema de educación bilingüe o, por lo menos, cursos de español como segunda lengua.

[a]*coloca... hangs up posters* [b]*fights* [c]*voice* [d]*such* [e]*laws*

Para escribir

Antes de escribir

Paso 1 Para esta actividad, vas a escribir una breve composición sobre los eventos más importantes en *Sol y viento* hasta el momento. Para comenzar, indica (✓) los eventos más importantes para narrar la historia. (Los espacios en blanco son para el **Paso 2.**)

_____ ☐ Jaime llegó a Santiago.

_____ ☐ Jaime conoció a (*met*) María en el Parque Forestal.

_____ ☐ Mario se ofreció (*offered himself*) como chofer.

_____ ☐ Jaime llamó a Carlos.

_____ ☐ Jaime conoció a Carlos.

_____ ☐ Jaime conoció a Yolanda, la esposa de Traimaqueo.

_____ ☐ Jaime supo (*found out*) que Carlos le había mentido (*had lied to him*).

_____ ☐ Jaime salió a correr.

_____ ☐ Carlos le sirvió a Jaime una copa de un vino especial.

_____ ☐ Jaime dio con (*ran into*) María otra vez.

_____ ☐ Traimaqueo le dio a Jaime una tour de la bodega y de la viña.

_____ ☐ Jaime invitó a María a tomar algo y ella aceptó.

Paso 2 Pon (*put*) los eventos que marcaste en orden cronológico. Escribe los números en los espacios en blanco del **Paso 1.**

A escribir

Paso 1 Usa los eventos de **Antes de escribir, Paso 1** para escribir un borrador (*rough draft*) en una hoja de papel aparte. Las palabras y expresiones a continuación pueden serte útiles.

al día siguiente	the next day
después	afterward
después de + (*noun/infinitive*)	after + (*noun/infinitive*)
entonces	then
luego	then
más tarde	later
pero	but
y	and

Paso 2 Mira bien lo que has escrito (*you have written*). ¿Quieres agregar (*to add*) oraciones para hacer la narración más interesante? Por ejemplo, en vez de decir: «Jaime fue al Parque Forestal para correr. Allí conoció a María», escribe algo como «Jaime fue a correr en el Parque Forestal donde conoció a María, una mujer joven, atractiva e inteligente».

Un día perfecto

Para pensar...

Basándote en las fotos, ¿por qué crees que este episodio se llama «Un día perfecto»? ¿Para quién o para quiénes es «perfecto» el día? ¿Quién es la mujer que habla con Carlos? ¿Dónde están? ¿De qué estarán hablando?[a]

[a]estarán... *must they be talking about*

SOL Y VIENTO

A primera vista

Antes de ver el episodio

Actividad A ¿Qué recuerdas?

¿Recuerdas lo que viste en el **Episodio 4**? Indica si las oraciones a continuación son ciertas o falsas. Si la oración es falsa, cámbiala.

	CIERTO	FALSO
1. Jaime pudo conocer a doña Isabel.	☐	☐
2. Carlos le regaló a Jaime una botella de vino.	☐	☐
3. Diego no sabe si va a continuar con sus estudios por presiones familiares.	☐	☐
4. La figura que compró Jaime simboliza un espíritu azteca.	☐	☐
5. Jaime y María quedaron en reunirse en el bar del hotel de Jaime.	☐	☐

Actividad B Vocabulario útil

Paso 1 Estudia las siguientes palabras y frases.

la Bolsa (de valores)	stock market
el brindis / brindemos	toast (*when drinking*) / let's toast
los campesinos	farm workers
las exportaciones	exports
los remolinos	pinwheels
te encargaste de	you took over, assumed responsibility for
Ud. no se limita a	you don't limit yourself to
vamos a tutearnos	let's use the **tú** form with each other

Paso 2 Usa las palabras y frases del **Paso 1** para completar cada oración a continuación. ¡**OJO**! No se usan todas las palabras y frases.

1. _____ trabajan la tierra.

2. _____ puede cambiar rápidamente.

3. ¿_____ los asuntos financieros de la compañía?

4. _____ por la salud y por los amigos.

5. _____ porque no me gusta ser tan formal.

Nota sobre el lenguaje

If you haven't yet learned the formation of the imperfect, another past tense in Spanish, here is a quick guide for talking about what someone *was doing* or what *was going on* before another event occurred in the past:

-ar verbs end in **-aba: hablaba** (*he/she was speaking*), **caminaba** (*he/she was walking*)

-er/-ir verbs end in **-ía: corría** (*he/she was running*), **salía** (*he/she was leaving*)

There are only three irregular verbs in the imperfect: **ir, ser,** and **ver.** To talk about what someone was doing or what was going on using these verbs, the forms are **iba (ir), era (ser),** and **veía (ver).** You will learn more about the imperfect throughout your study of Spanish.

Actividad C ¿Qué falta?

A continuación hay parte de una conversación entre doña Isabel y Carlos que no has visto (*that you haven't seen*). Antes de ver el episodio, escoge la opción apropiada para llenar cada espacio en blanco.

CARLOS: Mamá, ¿qué te parecería si vendiéramos[a] la viña?

ISABEL: ¿Vender «Sol y viento»? ¿Tú sabes cuánto _____¹ tu papá, cuánto _____² yo, para tener esta viña? ¡_____³ este país sin nada!

[a]¿qué... how would you feel if we sold

1. **a.** trabajaba   **b.** trabajó   **c.** trabaja
2. **a.** trabajaba   **b.** trabajé   **c.** trabajo
3. **a.** Vinimos a   **b.** Vivimos en   **c.** Salimos de

Actividad D El episodio

Ahora mira el episodio. Si hay algo que no entiendes bien, puedes volver a ver la escena en cuestión.

Después de ver el episodio

Actividad A ¿Qué recuerdas?

Contesta cada pregunta según lo que recuerdas del episodio.

1. ¿Qué hacía Jaime mientras esperaba a María?
   a. Hablaba por teléfono con Andy.
   b. Leía un artículo en el periódico.
2. Jaime piensa que María tiene una vida más interesante que la suya.
   a. cierto   **b.** falso
3. ¿Con quién habló Isabel después de la salida (*exit*) de Carlos?

4. ¿Qué significa la palabra **mapuche**?

5. ¿En qué trabajaba Jaime en su juventud?

　　a. Trabajaba en la exportación de los vinos.

　　b. Trabajaba en la fermentación de los vinos.

6. María tiene muchos amigos norteamericanos.

　　a. cierto　　**b.** falso

7. ¿Por qué colgó (*hung up*) el teléfono Jaime mientras hablaba con Andy?

　　a. Porque había una mala conexión.

　　b. Porque no quería seguir hablando con Andy.

Actividad B　¿Lo captaste?

Ahora verifica tus respuestas a la **Actividad C** en **Antes de ver el episodio.** Puedes ver esa escena de nuevo si quieres.

Actividad C　En resumen

Completa la siguiente narración con las palabras y expresiones apropiadas de la lista a la derecha.

En este episodio, las cosas _____[1] con la viña. Carlos le dice a su madre que _____[2] «Sol y viento», pero a doña Isabel _____[3] la idea.

　　Mientras tanto,[a] Jaime y María _____[4] la tarde juntos. Hablan de sus profesiones y a Jaime _____[5] el trabajo de María es más interesante que el suyo. Mientras toman una copa de vino, Jaime _____[6] a María por qué sabe tanto de los vinos. Las cosas _____[7] entre ellos hasta que María recibe una llamada de Diego y tiene que salir. Pero antes de despedirse[b] _____[8] un beso[c] a Jaime.

le cuenta
le da
le parece que
no le gusta nada
no van bien
pasan
quiere vender
van bien

[a]Mientras... *In the meantime*　[b]*saying good-bye*　[c]*kiss*

A segunda vista

Antes de ver el episodio

Actividad A ¡A escuchar!

En un momento, vas a ver el **Episodio 5** de nuevo. Repasa la siguiente escena. Luego, mientras la ves, completa lo que dicen los personajes con las palabras que faltan.

ISABEL: ¡Hijo! Me _____[1] dormida. ¿Te _____[2] algo, hijo?
CARLOS: No, nada. ¿Por qué?
ISABEL: Sí, algo te _____.[3] Soy tu mamá y te _____[4] mejor que nadie.
CARLOS: Entonces sabrás[a] que _____[5] mucho trabajo con la viña, mamá.
ISABEL: Cuando _____[6] tu papá, te _____[7] de los negocios. Yo ya _____[8] vieja y tu hermana _____[9] otros intereses.

[a]*you should know*

Actividad B El episodio

Ahora mira el episodio. No te olvides de hacer la **Actividad A** mientras lo ves. Puedes mirar el episodio más de una vez si quieres.

Después de ver el episodio

Actividad Intercambio

Paso 1 En este episodio conociste a doña Isabel, la madre de Carlos. Piensa en lo siguiente y contesta las preguntas según tu propia opinión

1. Doña Isabel le dijo a su hijo que había venido (*she had come*) a Chile sin nada. ¿De dónde vino, originalmente?
2. ¿Por qué no quiere vender la viña doña Isabel?
3. ¿Crees que doña Isabel debe hacer lo que quiere su hijo? ¿Por qué sí o por qué no?

Paso 2 Basándote en las respuestas del **Paso 1**, ¿qué adjetivos usarías (*would you use*) para describir a doña Isabel?

Detrás de la cámara

Did you notice who kissed whom first in this episode? As you have seen in previous episodes, Jaime is someone who likes to be in control of situations; however, his budding relationship with María is different. She seems to be the one in control. Although Jaime is not used to a woman taking the initiative in relationships, he doesn't complain!

SOL Y VIENTO: Enfoque cultural

En el **Episodio 5** viste un parque con una estatua enorme de la Virgen María. Los habitantes de Chile son, en su mayoría, católicos, como en la mayoría de los demás países hispanos. Por ejemplo, en España el 94% de la población es católica; en Chile, el 89%; en Venezuela, el 96%; y en Puerto Rico, el 85%.* Hasta en la Guinea Ecuatorial, donde hay una fuerte influencia de las culturas africanas, la mayoría de las personas se identifica con la Iglesia católica. Compara esas cifras[a] con el número de personas estadounidenses que se identifican como católicos: sólo llega al 28%. Claro, la manera en que se practica el catolicismo varía de país a país. Por ejemplo, en México la devoción a la Virgen de Guadalupe es casi más fuerte que la devoción a Jesucristo. Y en la zona andina (el Perú, Bolivia, el Ecuador) los indígenas han forjado[b] un catolicismo con restos[c] de la mitología y creencias de sus antepasados,[d] los inca.

▲ La estatua de la Virgen María en el Cerro San Cristóbal en Santiago.

[a]*numbers* [b]*han... have created* [c]*remnants* [d]*ancestors*

Para escribir

✱

Antes de escribir

Paso 1 Para esta actividad, vas a escribir una breve composición sobre los eventos del día perfecto desde el punto de vista (*point of view*) de María o de Jaime. Para comenzar, indica quién de los dos diría (*would say*) las siguientes oraciones. **¡OJO!** En algunos casos puede ser los dos. (Los espacios en blanco son para el **Paso 2.**)

		JAIME	MARÍA
1.	___ La esperaba (*I was waiting*) en la entrada (*entrance*) del funicular.	☐	☐
2.	___ Leía un artículo con mi foto cuando llegué.	☐	☐
3.	___ ¡Me besó (*kissed*)!	☐	☐
4.	___ Se me olvidó (*I forgot*) por completo mi cita con Diego.	☐	☐
5.	___ Pensé que tenía otro novio (*boyfriend*).	☐	☐
6.	___ Tomamos una copa de vino y hablamos un poco de mi familia.	☐	☐
7.	___ Lo pasábamos muy bien cuando llamó Diego.	☐	☐
8.	___ Tuvo que salir.	☐	☐

*C.I.A. World Fact Book, 2003.

		JAIME	MARÍA
9.	___ Fue un día perfecto.	☐	☐
10.	___ Su trabajo me parecía muy interesante.	☐	☐
11.	___ Mientras subíamos en el funicular hablábamos de su trabajo y del mío.	☐	☐

Paso 2 Ahora decide si vas a narrar los eventos del día desde la perspectiva de Jaime o de María. Primero, pon los eventos del **Paso 1** en orden cronológico. Escribe los números en los espacios en blanco del **Paso 1**.

A escribir

Paso 1 Usa los eventos del **Paso 1** de **Antes de escribir** para escribir un borrador en una hoja de papel aparte. Puedes utilizar las oraciones del personaje que *no* elegiste para dar más información, pero recuerda que vas a tener que cambiar algunos pronombres y verbos. Las palabras y expresiones a continuación pueden serte útiles.

de repente	suddenly
desafortunadamente	unfortunately
después	afterward
después de + (*noun/infinitive*)	after + (*noun/infinitive*)
entonces	then
luego	then
más tarde	later
pero	but
por fin	finally
y	and

Paso 2 Mira bien lo que has escrito. ¿Quieres agregar palabras, expresiones u oraciones para hacer la narración más interesante?

Confrontación

Para pensar...

En una de las fotos, María está por abrazar a^a un hombre. ¿Quién es ese hombre con María? ¿Cuál es su relación con ella?

En otra foto, Jaime está hablando con doña Isabel Sánchez. ¿Crees que a ella le cae bien^b la idea de vender la viña?

En otra foto, María se enoja^c con Jaime. ¿Por qué crees que está enojada María? ¿Qué ha hecho^d Jaime?

^aestá... *is about to hug* ^ba... *she likes* ^cse... *gets angry* ^dha... *has done*

SOL Y VIENTO

A primera vista

Antes de ver el episodio

Actividad A ¿Qué recuerdas?

Indica si las siguientes oraciones sobre la trama (*plot*) de *Sol y viento* son ciertas o falsas.

	C	F
1. María trabaja por los derechos de la comunidad mapuche.	☐	☐
2. Los padres de Jaime también eran personas de negocios.	☐	☐
3. Doña Isabel está de acuerdo con Carlos en vender la viña porque es demasiado (*too much*) trabajo mantenerla (*to maintain it*).	☐	☐
4. Carlos cree que la familia lo obligó a encargarse de (*take over*) la viña.	☐	☐
5. María y Jaime lo pasaron muy bien en la cita.	☐	☐

Detrás de la cámara

In **Episodio 6** of *Sol y viento* you will meet don Francisco (Paco) Aguilar, an old friend of the Sánchez family and owner of a fine restaurant in Mexico City. In addition to being a restaurateur, don Paco is also a distributor of fine wines. His job is to make contacts with wineries throughout the world and import their products into Mexico. He established a relationship with the Sánchez family many years ago on a trip through the Maipo Valley. He was so impressed with the wine produced at Sol y viento that he made it the house wine at his establishment.

Nota sobre el lenguaje

By now you have seen many command forms, both formal and informal as well as affirmative and negative. If you haven't yet learned the formation of commands, here is a quick guide, using the verb **hablar**. Note how in some instances the "opposite" vowel is used at the end of the verb (a → e, e/i → a).

	AFFIRMATIVE	NEGATIVE
tú	Habl**a** más fuerte.	No habl**es** tan fuerte.
vosotros/as	Habl**ad** más fuerte.	No habl**éis** tan fuerte.
Ud.	Habl**e** más fuerte.	No habl**e** tan fuerte.
Uds.	Habl**en** más fuerte.	No habl**en** tan fuerte.

In the preceding examples, the affirmative commands all mean *Speak louder,* whereas the negative commands mean *Don't speak so loudly.*

There are also many irregular forms for both formal and informal affirmative and negative commands, which you will learn throughout your study of Spanish.

Actividad B Vocabulario útil

Paso 1 Estudia las siguientes palabras y frases.

¡así me gustan!	that's how I like them!
déme...	give me . . .
el jitomate	a type of red tomato (*Mex.*)
el mercado	market
¡pruébelos!	try them!
¿qué tal están... ?	how are . . . ?
¡Ud. debería de saber!	You should know!

Paso 2 Usa las palabras y frases del **Paso 1** para completar el diálogo entre un mesero (*waiter*) y un cliente **¡OJO!** No se usan todas las palabras y frases.

MESERO: ¡Bienvenido,[a] don Pedro! ¿Le gustaría[b] pedir algo?

CLIENTE: ¡Claro que sí! El menú dice que hoy tienen _____[1] rellenos[c] como especialidad de la casa.

MESERO: Es cierto. ¿Los quiere pedir?

CLIENTE: Hmm... _____[2]

MESERO: Están bien deliciosos. El chef los prepara con una salsa picante[d] pero sabrosa.[e] _____[3]

CLIENTE: Está bien. Me ha convencido.[f] _____[4] la especialidad de la casa, por favor.

[a]*Welcome* [b]*¿Le... Would you like* [c]*stuffed* [d]*spicy* [e]*tasty* [f]*Me... You've convinced me.*

Actividad C ¿Qué falta?

A continuación hay un fragmento de una conversación telefónica que tiene don Paco.

PACO: ¿Bueno?[a]... ¿Bueno?... ¡Si no lo oigo bien! ¡_____[1] más fuerte!... ¿Bueno?... ¿Bueno?... Sí, _____[2] tantito[b]... ¿Bueno?... ¿Con quién?... ¡Ah, Isabel! ¡Qué sorpresa!

[a]*Hello? (Mex.)* [b]*a second (coll.)*

Escoge entre las palabras que siguen la más apropiada para cada espacio en blanco.

1. **a.** Hable
   b. Habla
2. **a.** espérame
   b. espéreme

Actividad D El episodio

Ahora mira el episodio. Si hay algo que no entiendes bien, puedes volver a ver la escena en cuestión.

Después de ver el episodio

Actividad A ¿Qué recuerdas?

Contesta cada pregunta a continuación según lo que recuerdas del episodio.

1. ¿A quién llama por teléfono doña Isabel?
   a. a Jaime, en su hotel   **b.** a don Paco, en México
2. ¿Cuál es la relación entre don Paco y María?
   a. Son amigos.   **b.** Son parientes.
3. Jaime se da cuenta de que María y Carlos son _____.
   a. primos   **b.** hermanos   **c.** cuñados
4. Jaime está harto de (*fed up with*) los pretextos (*excuses*) de Carlos y demanda _____ de la familia.
   a. las bodegas   **b.** las firmas   **c.** las cosechas
5. María comprende que Jaime no sabía quién era Carlos y lo perdona.
   a. cierto   **b.** falso

Actividad B ¿Lo captaste?

Vuelve a la **Actividad C** de **Antes de ver el episodio** para verificar tus respuestas. Si es necesario, vuelve a ver la escena en cuestión.

Actividad C Utilizando el contexto

Paso 1 Ya sabes que la frase **¿Qué tal?** es un saludo que quiere decir algo como *How's it going?* Repasa lo que dice don Paco en el mercado a continuación. ¿Qué crees que significa **¿Qué tal... ?** en este contexto?

PACO: ¡Buenas, doña Lourdes! ¿*Qué tal* están sus jitomates hoy?

Paso 2 A diferencia de otros hispanos, los mexicanos dicen **¿Bueno?** al contestar el teléfono. ¿Qué dice Jaime cuando contesta su teléfono celular?

Actividad D En resumen

Llena los espacios en blanco con las palabras a la derecha para completar el resumen del episodio que acabas de ver (*you just saw*).

En este episodio, doña Isabel _____[1] por lo que pasa en la viña. Por eso le pide ayuda a don Francisco (Paco) Aguilar, un amigo de la familia que vive en México. Se nota que a María _____[2] su «tío» Paco y que _____[3] mucho. Entretanto,[a] Jaime va a la viña donde _____[4] doña Isabel, la madre de Carlos. Doña Isabel afirma que «Sol y viento» no _____[5] y Jaime y Carlos entran en una conversación agitada. Luego, María llega del _____[6] con don Paco y presencia[b] la confrontación. Pensando que Jaime la está engañando,[c] María se enoja[d] y deja caer[e] _____[7] que Jaime le regaló.

aeropuerto
el amuleto
conoce a
está a la venta
está preocupada (*worried*)
le cae bien
lo respeta

[a]*Meanwhile* [b]*she witnesses* [c]*deceiving* [d]*se... gets angry* [e]*deja... drops*

A segunda vista

Antes de ver el episodio

Actividad A ¡A escuchar!

Repasa brevemente el siguiente fragmento de un diálogo entre Jaime y Carlos. Llena los espacios en blanco con las palabras correctas mientras ves el episodio.

> JAIME: ¡Esta cosa no va a funcionar! _____¹ prometió[a] las firmas de su madre, de su hermana y de los vecinos. ¡A que _____² ha hecho nada con la comunidad mapuche! Así es, ¿no? ¡La verdad es que no tiene nada! ¡Mi compañía quiere estas _____³!
>
> CARLOS: Por favor, _____⁴ un par de días más. Se las voy a conseguir.
>
> JAIME: Tenemos que firmar el contrato esta semana... ¡y Ud. no tiene la influencia _____⁵!
>
> CARLOS: Ya _____:⁶ yo voy a convencer a mi madre ¡y a mi _____⁷ lo da lo mismo![b]
>
> JAIME: ¡Lo dudo![c] Según lo que _____⁸ y he oído, ¡pienso que a su hermana sí le _____⁹ el destino de estas tierras!

[a]*you promised* [b]*le... doesn't care* [c]*I doubt*

Actividad B El episodio

Ahora vas a ver el episodio de nuevo. Presta atención especial a la escena en que Carlos y Jaime discuten (*argue*) y apunta las palabras que faltan para la **Actividad A.** Puedes mirar el episodio más de una vez si quieres.

Después de ver el episodio

Actividad Intercambio

Ya sabes que Jaime y María tuvieron una confrontación horrible. Contesta las siguientes preguntas.

1. ¿Qué crees que piensa María de la relación entre su hermano y Jaime? ¿De quién sospecha (*is she suspicious*) más, de Carlos o de Jaime?
2. ¿Cuál crees que es la causa principal de su enojo (*anger*), la venta de las tierras familiares? ¿las consecuencias de la venta para los mapuches? ¿la decepción que siente con respecto a Jaime?
3. ¿Cómo puede resolverse esta situación difícil? Apunten algunas ideas.

EPISODIO 6 ✳ CONFRONTACIÓN

Detrás de la cámara

Another reason Jaime is so successful at what he does is that he doesn't wait for things to happen—he makes them happen. Jaime quickly gets the hint that Carlos has no real game plan for getting his mother and sister to sign the contract. When he finds out from Traimaqueo that Carlos's mother, doña Isabel, was in the house all along and not in Santiago as Carlos had told him, he circumvents Carlos altogether and goes straight to doña Isabel. Suspecting something is awry, doña Isabel agrees to speak to him.

SOL Y VIENTO: Enfoque cultural

Has visto que en el **Episodio 6,** Jaime le dice a Carlos: «¡A que tampoco ha hecho nada con la comunidad mapuche!» Evidentemente, Carlos había prometido[a] conseguir las tierras de los mapuches que vivían en la zona. En cambio,[b] su hermana María lucha[c] por esa comunidad indígena para preservar su cultura.

El indigenismo y los derechos de los indígenas en Latinoamérica son temas muy importantes en muchos países como el Perú, Chile, México y otros. Por seis siglos los indígenas han sufrido discriminación que los ha mantenido en las capas[d] más bajas de la sociedad. Afortunadamente, en el siglo XX empezó a demostrarse interés[e] en el indigenismo a través del arte del mexicano Diego Rivera y el novelista ecuatoriano Jorge Icaza, entre otros. En el Perú empezaron a reconocer la importancia de ofrecer a los indígenas educación en su lengua nativa, el quechua, y establecieron programas de educación bilingüe en el año 1972. Es más,[f] en 1979 la constitución peruana reconoció el español como lengua oficial del país, pero a la vez que el quechua forma parte integral de la cultura del país, y los dos idiomas quedaron como lenguas oficiales, con restricciones. Aun con estos avances, la situación no está completamente resuelta.[g] Por ejemplo, en 1994 los indígenas del estado mexicano de Chiapas se sublevaron[h] contra el gobierno, reclamando más tierra y más inclusión en el sistema político. Seguramente, la situación de los grupos minoritarios indígenas seguirá siendo[i] un tema central en varios países hispanos por muchos años.

▲ El indigenismo sigue siendo un tema central en la vida de los indígenas, como estas en el Ecuador.

[a]*promised* [b]*En... On the other hand* [c]*fights* [d]*layers* [e]*empezó... interest began to appear* [f]*Es... What's more* [g]*resolved* [h]*se... rose up* [i]*seguirá... will continue to be*

Para escribir

✳

Antes de escribir

Para esta actividad, vas a escribir una composición sobre los eventos más importantes que han ocurrido entre Jaime y María hasta el momento. Describe cómo se sentían (*felt*) Jaime y María en cada situación a continuación.

MODELO: Jaime conoció a María. →
Jaime estaba cansado de correr, pero estaba muy contento. María se sentía... porque...

1. Jaime se chocó con María en el parque.

   _____

2. Jaime vio a María cuando fue de compras en el mercado.

   _____

3. María y Jaime tomaron vino en el café al aire libre (*outdoor*).

   _____

4. María tiró al suelo (*threw down*) el amuleto que Jaime le regaló.

   _____

A escribir

Paso 1 Usa la información de **Antes de ver el episodio** para escribir un borrador en una hoja de papel aparte. Las palabras y expresiones a continuación pueden serte útiles.

a la vez	at the same time
además (de)	in addition (to)
después	afterward
entonces	then
luego	then
más tarde	later
mientras	while
por lo tanto	therefore

Paso 2 Mira bien lo que has escrito. ¿Quieres agregar palabras, expresiones u oraciones para hacer la narración más interesante?

Bajo el sol

Para pensar...

En una de las fotos Jaime y Mario sufren un pequeño accidente. ¿Adónde iban? ¿Qué les pasó?

En otras fotos Jaime está con doña Isabel y don Paco. ¿Crees que les ha convencido Jaime[a] a vender la viña? ¿Qué crees que pasa en la escena? ¿Están todos contentos?

[a]les... Jaime has convinced them

SOL Y VIENTO

A primera vista

Antes de ver el episodio

Actividad A ¿Qué recuerdas?

Indica si las siguientes oraciones son ciertas o falsas, según lo que sabes de la trama (*plot*) de *Sol y viento*.

	CIERTO	FALSO
1. Don Paco es dueño de un restaurante en Chile.	☐	☐
2. El esposo de doña Isabel ya ha muerto.	☐	☐
3. Doña Isabel llama a don Paco porque se preocupa por la viña.	☐	☐
4. Ahora Jaime sabe que Carlos y María son hermanos.	☐	☐
5. María sigue respetando a Jaime aunque sabe que trabaja para Bartel Aquapower.	☐	☐

Actividad B Vocabulario útil

Paso 1 Estudia las siguientes palabras y frases.

arregla	(he) fixes
atraviesa por	(one) travels through
los hechos	deeds
pinchó / ponchó*	(it) punctured
la represa	dam
el repuesto	spare tire
la rueda	tire

Paso 2 Usa las palabras del **Paso 1** para completar cada oración a continuación. **¡OJO!** No se usan todas las palabras y frases.

1. Hoover es el nombre de una _____ grande en los Estados Unidos.
2. Michelin y Goodyear son marcas (*brand names*) populares de _____.
3. Para ir en coche de Los Ángeles, California, a Las Vegas, Nevada, uno _____ el desierto Mojave.
4. La rueda que se saca del baúl (*trunk*) de un auto en casos de emergencia es _____.
5. Generalmente _____ de una persona influyen mucho en nuestra opinión de esa persona.

---

*The use of **pinchar** (by Mario) and **ponchar** (by Jaime) is just one example of many dialectical differences that exist in the Spanish-speaking world.

Actividad C   ¿Qué falta?

En el **Episodio 7** Jaime y Mario van a hablar del tiempo que falta para llegar a «Sol y viento». Llena los espacios en blanco con las opciones a continuación. Puedes verificar tus respuestas después de ver el episodio.

JAIME: ¿Estamos lejos?
MARIO: En automóvil, a siete minutos. A pie, cuarenta y cinco minutos, más o menos. Menos si se toma _____[1] por ahí...
JAIME: Me voy a pie. Nos vemos en la viña.
MARIO: ¡Don Jaime! ¡El sol está picando fuerte![a] ¡Que no le dé _____[2]!

1. **a.** la autopista (*highway*)
   b. un atajo (*shortcut*)
2. **a.** un infarto (*heart attack*)
   b. una insolación (*heatstroke*)

[a]picando... *really beating down*

Actividad D   El episodio

Ahora mira el episodio. Si hay alguna escena que no entiendes bien, vuelve a verla.

Después de ver el episodio

Actividad A   ¿Qué recuerdas?

Contesta las preguntas a continuación según lo que recuerdas del **Episodio 7**.

1. Mario no pudo arreglar la rueda pinchada porque no tenía...
   a. herramientas (*tools*)   **b.** gato (*tire jack*)   **c.** repuesto
2. Jaime sufrió una insolación antes de llegar a la casa de los Sánchez. ¿Cierto o falso?
   a. cierto   **b.** falso
3. Según don Paco, Bartel Aquapower hizo mucho daño a la ecología de este país.
   a. el Brasil   **b.** Bulgaria   **c.** Bolivia
4. Jaime renuncia a (*quits*) su trabajo con Bartel Aquapower. ¿Cierto o falso?
   a. cierto   **b.** falso
5. Doña Isabel le dijo a Jaime que María no _____ fácilmente.
   a. se enamora   **b.** perdona   **c.** se divierte

Actividad B   ¿Lo captaste?

Vuelve a la **Actividad C** de **Antes de ver el episodio** para verificar tus respuestas. Si es necesario, vuelve a ver la escena en cuestión.

Have you noticed that while María and Jaime switched to the use of **tú** in a previous episode, Mario has continued to use **usted** with Jaime? Even though Mario feels the need to comment on María and Jaime's relationship, he and Jaime are not friends and are not of the same age group. Mario is, in effect, an employee of Jaime's. However, Jaime does use **tú** when addressing Mario. You may also have noticed that Traimaqueo uses **tú** with Carlos, although he is technically employed by the family. What is different here is that Traimaqueo has known Carlos since the latter was a little boy. The use of **tú** was natural in that adult–child relationship. That Traimaqueo now works for Carlos has not changed that fundamental and earlier pattern of interaction. María, of course, when finding out what Jaime has been up to, immediately drops the **tú** and reverts to **usted**. Did you catch this in the previous episode?

Actividad C En resumen

Llena los espacios en blanco con las palabras a la derecha para completar el resumen del **Episodio 7.**

En este episodio, a Mario y Jaime _____[1] una rueda camino a la viña. Como Mario no tenía _____,[2] Jaime decidió seguir a pie. En ruta a la viña, Jaime sufrió una _____[3] y se desmayó.[a] Mientras Jaime se recuperaba en casa de doña Isabel, don Paco _____[4] que Bartel Aquapower quería construir una represa en el valle, lo cual le haría[b] mucho daño tanto al medio ambiente como a _____[5] mapuche. Jaime comprendió el error de _____[6] y en una conversación con Andy, renunció a su trabajo con Bartel Aquapower.

la comunidad
insolación
le informó
repuesto
se les pinchó
sus acciones

[a]*se... he passed out* [b]*would cause*

Nota sobre el lenguaje

If you haven't yet studied the subjunctive mood, here is a quick guide on forming the subjunctive and one of its most common uses.

Forms

To form the present subjunctive, use the "opposite" vowel in verb endings, modeled after the **yo** form of the verb in the present indicative.

tomar: tomo → tom-	=	tome, tomes, tome...
volver: vuelvo → vuelv-	=	vuelva, vuelvas, vuelva...
pedir: pido → pid-	=	pida, pidas, pida...
conocer: conozco → conozc-	=	conozca, conozcas, conozca...
decir: digo → dig-	=	diga, digas, diga...

There are also irregular subjunctive forms, such as **dé (dar), esté (estar), vaya (ir), sepa (saber),** and **sea (ser).**

Uses

One of the most common uses of the subjunctive is to express will, desire, or volition (you want someone to do something or you want something to happen). The subjunctive is used because that action exists only in your mind; it hasn't yet happened. Here are a couple of examples.

Quiero que me busques un libro sobre Cervantes.
I want you to look for a book on Cervantes for me.

Espero que vengas a la fiesta el sábado.
I hope you come to the party on Saturday.

You will learn more about the subjunctive throughout your study of Spanish.

A segunda vista

Antes de ver el episodio

Actividad A ¡A escuchar!

Repasa el siguiente fragmento de la conversación entre doña Isabel, Jaime y don Paco. En unos momentos vas a escuchar la conversación y llenar los espacios en blanco con las palabras correctas. ¡No vuelvas a leer otros fragmentos de este episodio!

    ISABEL: ¿María Teresa _____ [1]?
               ¡Huy! ¡Es durísima! Va a
               ser muy difícil...
               _____ [2] Ud., don Jaime, merezca su perdón.
    JAIME: Entiendo que será[a] difícil y quizás[b] no me
               _____ [3] su perdón, pero...

[a]*it will be* [b]*perhaps*

Actividad B El episodio

Ahora vas a ver el episodio de nuevo. Presta atención especial a la escena en que doña Isabel y don Paco hablan con Jaime en la casa y apunta las palabras que faltan para la **Actividad A.** Puedes mirar el episodio más de una vez si quieres.

Después de ver el episodio

Actividad Intercambio

La familia Sánchez ya sabe que Carlos quiere vender la viña. ¿Por qué crees que quiere venderla si la viña ha tenido tanto éxito? (Recuerda que hace muchos años que Carlos es administrador y que la producción ha sido de muy buena calidad.) ¿Crees que Carlos va a revelar sus intenciones o que va a seguir engañando a la familia? Apunta algunas ideas sobre los posibles motivos de Carlos y lo que crees que va a pasar con él.

Detrás de la cámara

You have seen Isabel in a few scenes, and you probably have some idea about the type of person she is. Isabel is compassionate but also strong-willed and cares deeply about her family, the community, and, of course, the winery. After she immigrated with her husband from Spain to Chile, they built a prosperous winery from the ground up. Now an aging widow, Isabel is not in very good health. Despite her frailty, she is not afraid to speak her mind nor is she easily persuaded to do anything against her wishes. In a sense, she is typical of the "strong women" often portrayed by Katherine Hepburn, Bette Davis, and others in the glamour era of the silver screen. Can you think of any other movie characters who are like her?

En el **Episodio 7** Paco menciona el Internet. La imagen que muchas personas tienen de los países hispanos es una de países pobres, del «tercer mundo» y con poca modernización. En general, los países hispanos no gozan de[a] los excesos tecnológicos de una cultura como la de este país, pero no son tan atrasados[b] como algunos creen. España es tan moderna como cualquier otro país de Europa y las ciudades de Santiago, Buenos Aires, Caracas, México, D.F. y San Juan, entre otras, ofrecen casi todo lo que se podría[c] encontrar en las grandes ciudades norteamericanas. Por ejemplo, hay «cibercafés» donde la gente va para tomar un café y leer su correo electrónico. También, los negocios y bancos están tan bien equipados de tecnología como cualquier negocio en este país. Además, la viña donde se filmó *Sol y viento* poseía de[d] todo lo moderno como cualquier viña en Napa o Sonoma, California, por ejemplo. Finalmente, varios Premios Nóbel de Ciencia se han ortogado[e] a científicos de países hispanos. Claro, en las zonas rurales es un poco diferente, pero ¿no es así en casi cualquier país del mundo?

▲ Los cibercafés, como este en México, D.F., son muy populares en todas partes del mundo.

[a]no... *don't enjoy*   [b]*backward*   [c]*se... one could*   [d]*poseía... possessed*   [e]*awarded*

Para escribir

*

Antes de escribir

Paso 1 Hasta ahora sabemos muy poco del pasado de Carlos Sánchez. Para esta actividad, vas a inventar una breve historia en la que describes el pasado de Carlos. Para comenzar, contesta las preguntas a continuación. No hay respuestas correctas; son tus opiniones.

1. ¿Cuántos años tenía Carlos cuando murió su papá? ¿Qué hacía Carlos en esa época? ¿trabajaba? ¿estudiaba? ¿vivía en la viña?

_____

_____

2. Siendo el único hijo varón (*male*), ¿qué responsabilidades, en cuanto a la familia y el manejo (*management*) de la viña, le tocaban a la muerte de su padre?

_____

_____

3. ¿Quería Carlos encargarse de la viña? Si dices que sí, explica por qué era importante para él asumir (*to assume*) este puesto. Si dices que no, ¿qué quería hacer con su vida? ¿Quería casarse? ¿tener hijos? ¿seguir otra profesión?

_____

_____

4. ¿De adolescentes, se llevaban bien Carlos y María? ¿Cómo reaccionó Carlos cuando María decidió trabajar en un campo (*field*) que no fuera (*that wasn't*) la viña?

_____

_____

5. Explica cómo eran las relaciones entre Carlos y Paco tras (*after*) la muerte del padre de Carlos. ¿Lo trataba Paco como si fuera (*as if he were*) su propio hijo? ¿Le ayudaba en los asuntos de la viña? ¿Crees que Carlos respetaba a Paco o que resentía algo de él?

_____

_____

6. Explica las circunstancias que llevaron a Carlos a querer vender la viña. ¿Estaba cansado del trabajo? ¿aburrido? ¿Resentía algo de su familia? ¿Había otros problemas?

_____

_____

A escribir

Paso 1 Usa tus respuestas de **Antes de ver el episodio** para escribir un borrador en una hoja de papel aparte. Las palabras y expresiones a continuación pueden serte útiles.

además (de)	in addition (to)
al contrario	on the contrary
así que	therefore
creo que	I think that
es obvio/evidente que	it's obvious/evident that
me parece que	it seems to me that
opino que	it's my opinion that
por lo visto	apparently
sin embargo	however

Paso 2 Mira bien lo que has escrito. ¿Quieres agregar palabras, expresiones u oraciones para hacer la narración más interesante?

Sin alternativa

Para pensar...

¿Qué lee María cuando Carlos entra en la oficina? ¿Será[a] algo sobre los negocios de su hermano o una carta de Jaime? En otra foto, ¿de qué hablarán don Paco y María?[b] ¿Crees que don Paco trata de convencer a María que haga[c] algo? En la tercera foto, ¿de qué hablarán Carlos y doña Isabel? ¿Con cuál o cuáles de los fotos crees que está relacionado el título del episodio?

[a]Could it be   [b]hablarán... would don Paco and María be talking about   [c]que... that she do

SOL Y VIENTO

A primera vista

Antes de ver el episodio

Actividad A   ¿Qué recuerdas?

A continuación hay unas citas (*quotes*) de lo que han dicho ciertos personajes en el episodio previo. De los personajes a continuación, ¿puedes indicar quién lo dijo y a quién se lo dijo?

1. «¡El sol está picando fuerte!» _____ se lo dijo a _____.
2. «Ya le dije que esta tierra no se vende.» _____ se lo dijo a _____.
3. «¿Comprende el daño de una represa en la zona?» _____ se lo dijo a _____.
4. «Quizás no me merezca que me perdone.» _____ se lo dijo a _____.
5. «Si pasan cinco días más, no va el negocio.» _____ se lo dijo a _____.

Actividad B Vocabulario útil

Paso 1   Estudia las siguientes palabras y frases.

comprometer	to commit, get involved
confiar en	to trust
cumplir con	to follow through with
las deudas	debts
engañar	to deceive
fracasar	to fail
la inversión	investment
los invitados	guests
renunciar a	to quit
tramposo/a	swindler

Paso 2   Usa las palabras y frases del **Paso 1** para completar cada oración a continuación. **¡OJO!** No se usan todas las palabras y frases.

1. Muchos estudiantes universitarios tienen muchas _____ como la matrícula (*tuition*), el coche o las tarjetas de crédito.
2. Me gustaría _____ mi trabajo porque ya no me gusta nada.
3. ¿A quién quieres _____? Sé que no me dices la verdad.
4. ¿Cuántos _____ vienen a la fiesta?
5. Si no queremos _____ en este proyecto, tenemos que trabajar mucho.

Nota sobre el lenguaje

In Spanish, the present perfect is used to talk about something that *has happened*. If you haven't yet learned the present perfect, use a form of **haber** plus a past participle (**-ado, -ido**). **Haber** is an auxiliary verb that means *to have,* although it is *not* interchangeable with **tener**. It is also irregular in its forms. The first example in the **yo** form means *I have traveled.*

he	hemos	viajado
has	habéis	+ conocido
ha	han	vivido

There are also many irregular past participle forms, a few of which are **dicho (decir)**, **escrito (escribir)**, **hecho (hacer)**, and **visto (ver)**.

The past perfect is used to talk about what *had happened* at a specific point in the past. For the past perfect, use the imperfect of the verb **haber** and a past participle.

Había viajado a Chile antes de tomar este curso.
I had traveled to Chile before taking this course.

Actividad C   ¿Qué falta?

En este episodio, Isabel se enfrenta con (*confronts*) Carlos. Lee el diálogo.

ISABEL: ¡Aquí hay más deudas que en todo el tiempo de la administración de tu papá! ¿Qué has hecho con el dinero de «Sol y viento»?

CARLOS: Mamá, estos son tiempos diferentes. El negocio es mucho más difícil.

ISABEL: ¿Me crees tonta? ¿Qué hiciste con el dinero de «Sol y viento»?

CARLOS: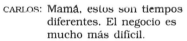

¿Qué crees que dice Carlos en el espacio en blanco?

a. Invertí las ganancias (*earnings*) de la viña en varias compañías de tecnología.
b. Me enteré (*I found out*) de que papá había muerto sin pagar muchas de sus deudas y las tuve que pagar yo.

Actividad D   El episodio

Ahora mira el episodio. Si hay algo que no entiendes bien, puedes volver a ver la escena en cuestión.

Después de ver el episodio

Actividad A ¿Qué recuerdas?

Contesta las siguientes preguntas sobre el **Episodio 8**.

1. Por fin Carlos le convence a María de que firme los papeles para vender «Sol y viento».

   a. cierto   **b.** falso

2. ¿Cuál fue la especialización de Jaime?

   a. economía   **b.** ecología   **c.** administración de empresas

3. ¿Quién invita a Jaime a la recepción de «Sol y viento»?

   a. don Paco   **b.** doña Isabel

4. ¿Qué hizo Carlos con el dinero de «Sol y viento»?

   a. Lo depositó en una cuenta de ahorros en el extranjero.

   b. Lo usó para pagar las deudas de su padre.

   c. Lo invirtió (*he invested*) en compañías de tecnología.

Actividad B ¿Lo captaste?

Verifica tus respuestas de la **Actividad C** en **Antes de ver el episodio**. Si es necesario, puedes ver el episodio de nuevo.

Actividad C Utilizando el contexto

¿Pudiste deducir el significado de las palabras y expresiones que aparecen en letra cursiva a continuación?

> YOLANDA: ¿Así vas a estar vestida para la recepción?
> MARÍA: No. Me voy a poner un vestido más tarde porque...
> YOLANDA: ¡*Deja!* Yo me encargo de las flores. *Mejor anda a cambiarte* ahora mismo. ¡Ya van a llegar los invitados!

Actividad D En resumen

Completa la siguiente narración con las palabras y expresiones apropiadas de la lista a la derecha.

En este episodio, María _____¹ que Carlos _____² al resto de la familia y a los vecinos. María _____³ explicaciones a su hermano, pero Carlos _____⁴ que sólo él _____⁵ el derecho de manejar los negocios de la viña. Luego, María _____⁶ a su madre. Entonces doña Isabel _____⁷ a su hijo qué _____⁸ con el dinero de la viña. Parece que Carlos _____⁹ en malas inversiones. A causa de este engaño, doña Isabel _____¹⁰ a su hijo dos opciones.

descubrió
engañaba
había hecho
le dio
le pidió
le preguntó
lo había perdido
respondió
se lo contó todo
tenía

A segunda vista

Antes de ver el episodio

Actividad A ¡A escuchar!

Repasa la siguiente escena. Luego, mientras ves el episodio, completa lo que dicen los personajes con las palabras y expresiones que oyes.

> MARÍA: ¿En serio? ¿Me _____[1] a hablar? ¿Cuándo? Yo creo que ibas a tratar de engañarme... ¡como _____[2] al señor Ayala para sacarle sus terrenos! ¿O acaso no es para eso que está aquí el señor Talavera, para _____[3] y sacarme una firma?
>
> CARLOS: ¿Ese inoportuno?[a] Ni siquiera[b] _____[4] que _____.[5] ¿Y desde cuándo te interesan los negocios de la viña «Sol y viento»? Nunca _____[6] nada. Ni siquiera sabes cómo funciona. ¿Tú crees que esto _____[7] solo?

[a]¿Ese... That guy? [b]even

Actividad B El episodio

Ahora mira el episodio. No te olvides de hacer la **Actividad A** mientras lo ves. Puedes mirar el episodio más de una vez si quieres.

Después de ver el episodio

Actividad Intercambio

¿Qué piensas de las opciones que le dio doña Isabel a Carlos? ¿Son justas (*fair*) o piensas que hay otra alternativa? ¿Piensas que Carlos va a aceptar las condiciones de su madre o va a rogarle (*beg her*) que él se quede en «Sol y viento»?

Detrás de la cámara

María sometimes feels guilty because she has moved away from home and is not regularly involved in the family business. Yet, when María asks her mother if she wishes that María had stayed at home to work in the vineyard, doña Isabel promptly says "no." Doña Isabel also says that she is proud that her daughter is a university professor. In spite of having moved away, María and her mother maintain a very close relationship, and doña Isabel does not worry at all about María. Although María can be stubborn at times, doña Isabel trusts her daughter, and she knows that María's intelligence and self-confidence serve her well.

SOL Y VIENTO: Enfoque cultural

En el **Episodio 8,** mientras todos se preparan para la recepción, María ayuda a Traimaqueo con algo bastante pesado.[a] Él le dice «¡Cuidado![b] ¡Cuidado! Ay, gracias, m'hija.[c]» Claro, ya sabes que María no es hija de Traimaqueo. Es muy común entre los hispanohablantes emplear de forma afectuosa los términos **hijo** o **hija** al dirigirse[d] a una persona más joven. **Tío** y **tía** son utilizados para demostrar cariño a una persona mayor, como lo hace María con don Paco. Paco es amigo de la familia —no es pariente— pero María lo quiere mucho, y por eso le dice **tío Paco.**

En el **Episodio 4** ya viste a Yolanda llamar a Traimaqueo **viejo.** Entre parejas, es frecuente que se llamen **viejo** o **vieja** como muestra de la intimidad y cariño entre ellos. Compara esto con el inglés, en que *my old lady* y *the old man* no son términos tan cariñosos. **Viejo** y **vieja** también se usan entre amigos íntimos y, a veces, entre otros miembros de la familia.

▲ ¿Crees que usa términos de cariño esta pareja tejana (de Texas)?

[a]*heavy* [b]*Careful!* [c]*mi hija* [d]*addressing*

Para escribir

Antes de escribir

Paso 1 Para esta actividad, vas a escribir sobre los factores que han contribuido al engaño de Carlos y si piensas que él merece otra oportunidad. Para comenzar, indica si estás de acuerdo o no con las siguientes afirmaciones sobre Carlos.

	ESTOY DE ACUERDO.	NO ESTOY DE ACUERDO.
1. Era muy machista (*male chauvinist*).	☐	☐
2. Sólo pensaba en sí mismo, no en los demás.	☐	☐
3. Se sintió obligado a quedarse a trabajar en la viña después de la muerte de su padre.	☐	☐
4. Invirtió dinero en compañías tecnológicas para su propio beneficio, no por el bien de la viña.	☐	☐
5. Trataba mal a sus empleados (como Traimaqueo) a causa de su propia inseguridad.	☐	☐
6. Le tenía mucha envidia (*envy*) a su hermana María.	☐	☐

	ESTOY DE ACUERDO.	NO ESTOY DE ACUERDO.
7. Pensaba que su madre quería más a María que a él.	☐	☐
8. Invirtió dinero para demostrar (*show*) a su familia que él también era inteligente.	☐	☐
9. Estaba resentido (*resentful*) por el éxito (*success*) profesional de su hermana.	☐	☐

Paso 2 Ahora indica si le darías otra oportunidad a Carlos para quedarse a trabajar en la viña. ¿Qué afirmaciones del **Paso 1** apoyan tu decisión? Piensa en tres argumentos más y escríbelos aquí.

1. _____

2. _____

3. _____

A escribir

Paso 1 Usa tus respuestas de **Antes de ver el episodio** para escribir un borrador en una hoja de papel aparte. Empieza tu composición con una de las siguientes oraciones:

☐ Si fuera (*If I were*) Isabel, le daría (*I would give*) otra oportunidad a Carlos.

☐ Si fuera Isabel, le daría a Carlos las mismas opciones que ella le dio.

Las palabras y expresiones a continuación pueden serte útiles.

además (de)	besides, in addition (to)
(no) lo merece	he deserves (doesn't deserve) it
por eso	that's why, therefore
por fin	finally
sin embargo	however

Paso 2 Mira bien lo que has escrito. ¿Quieren agregar palabras, expresiones u oraciones para hacer la narración más interesante?

Un brindis
por el futuro

Para pensar...

Como puedes ver en una de las fotos, doña Isabel se está dirigiendo a[a] los invitados que están presentes para degustar[b] la nueva cosecha. ¿Qué crees que les está diciendo? ¿Saben los invitados de los problemas de «Sol y viento»?

En otra foto, don Paco les habla a doña Isabel y a María. ¿Qué les cuenta? ¿Tiene una solución para salir de las deudas que contrajo[c] Carlos?

En otra foto, Jaime hace una visita al sitio de excavación donde trabaja María. ¿Qué crees que va a pasar? ¿Lo va a perdonar María? ¿Cómo se resuelven los conflictos presentes en la historia de *Sol y viento*?

[a]*se... is addressing* [b]*taste* [c]*acquired*

SOL Y VIENTO

A primera vista

Antes de ver el episodio

Actividad A ¿Qué recuerdas?

Contesta cada pregunta con información verdadera, según lo que sabes de *Sol y viento* hasta el momento.

1. ¿Qué palabra describe mejor la actitud de Carlos ante su hermana, María? ¿Está resentido, celoso o enojado Carlos?
2. ¿Cómo supo doña Isabel de los documentos falsificados por Carlos?
3. Jaime dijo que no lo invitaron a la recepción para degustar el vino. ¿Por qué fue, entonces?
4. Cuando doña Isabel confrontó a Carlos en el jardín, le dijo que le quedaban dos opciones. ¿Cuáles eran?
5. Al final del **Episodio 8,** don Paco dijo que María debía escuchar algo. ¿Qué debe escuchar?

Actividad B Vocabulario útil

Paso 1 Estudia las siguientes palabras y frases.

a lo mejor	probably
bienvenido/a	welcome (*adj.*)
hacerse cargo de	to take charge of
humilde	humble

Paso 2 Usa las palabras y frases del **Paso 1** para completar cada oración a continuación.

1. Los buenos amigos son siempre _____ a mi casa.
2. Yo tuve que _____ del asunto porque el señor García era mal administrador.
3. Soy bastante _____. No me gusta hablar de mí mismo.
4. _____ no lo sabes, pero esta mañana hubo un accidente en la oficina.

Nota sobre el lenguaje

If you haven't studied the future tense yet, you can recognize it because all verb forms, whether **-ar** or **-er/-ir,** end with the following: **-ré, -rás, -rá, -remos, -réis, -rán.**

> **tomaré:** *I will take*
>
> **comerán:** *they will eat*
>
> **vivirán:** *they will live*

Some common future verb forms have irregular stems (presented here in the **él/ella** form): **tendrá (tener), hará (hacer), podrá (poder),** and so forth.

Actividad C ¿Qué falta?

Lee la siguiente presentación (*introduction*) y brindis que da doña Isabel al principio del **Episodio 9.** ¿Puedes deducir las palabras y expresiones que faltan?

ISABEL: Señoras y señores: primero que nada, en nombre de mi _____,[1] quiero agradecer vuestra presencia en esta importante ocasión. Para la viña «Sol y viento», es un orgullo que Uds. la visiten. ¡Y espero que el vino que vamos a degustar esta noche _____[2] uno de los mejores que hayan probado en su vida! También les _____[3] presentar a don Francisco Aguilar, gran amigo de nuestra familia y apreciado socio[a] de la viña «Sol y viento». Él ha venido desde México a probar nuestro vino. Bueno, sin más, les quiero _____[4] nuestra nueva cosecha. ¡Salud!

[a]*partner*

Actividad D El episodio

Ahora mira el episodio. **¡OJO!** Sería buena idea *no* mirar todo el episodio y parar al final de la escena en donde degustan el vino. ¡Así guardas la última parte y el fin para **A segunda vista!**

Después de ver el episodio

Actividad A ¿Qué recuerdas?

Contesta cada pregunta según lo que recuerdas del episodio.

1. ¿Qué preguntas hacen los vecinos e invitados? ¿Qué rumores han oído?
2. Don Paco hace un anuncio en público que para la familia implica la salvación de la viña. ¿Qué anuncia él?

Detrás de la cámara

You probably noticed in **Episodio 8** of *Sol y viento* that María is not in total control of her destiny with Jaime. By inviting Jaime to the reception, don Paco and doña Isabel are conspiring to bring him and María together. They know that Jaime is right for María, even if she does not. As you approach the end of the movie, remember that *Sol y viento* is a story about harmony between the land and the peoples who inhabit it. In this story, individuals do not wholly control their destinies, and Jaime's and María's lives are part of a chain of inevitable events.

Actividad B ¿Lo captaste?

Verifica tus repuestas para la **Actividad C** en **Antes de ver el episodio.** Puedes volver a ver la escena si es necesario.

Actividad C Utilizando el contexto

Utiliza el contexto y la situación para deducir el significado de las expresiones en letra cursiva. Puedes volver a ver esa parte del episodio si quieres.

> INVITADA: Isabel, ¿qué hay de los rumores de que van a vender «Sol y viento»?
> INVITADO: Yo también escuché algo así. *¿Qué hay de cierto?*[1]
> ISABEL: *Mientras me quede un soplo de vida, ¡no le pasará nada a esta viña ni a estas tierras!*[2] *¡Aquí no se venderá nada!*[3]

1. ...   **2.** ...   **3.** ...

Actividad D En resumen

Completa la siguiente narración con las palabras y expresiones apropiadas de la lista a la derecha.

Ya sabes que, antes de comenzar la recepción para degustar el vino de la nueva cosecha de «Sol y viento», don Paco le habla a María. Le _____[1] que escuche a su corazón y que no se guíe solamente _____[2] su cerebro.

La degustación del vino empieza con una presentación de doña Isabel. _____[3] da a los invitados la bienvenida[a] y luego hace un brindis por la nueva cosecha. Después de probar el vino, algunos vecinos le preguntan sobre algunos rumores que circulan de que _____[4] la viña. Doña Isabel, con aire de mujer decidida, dice: «_____[5] me quede un soplo de vida, no se venderá nada.»

dice
les
mientras
por
se vende

[a]da... *she welcomes the guests*

A segunda vista

Antes de ver el episodio

Actividad A ¡A escuchar!

Repasa la siguiente escena. Luego, mientras ves el episodio, completa lo que dicen los personajes con las palabras y expresiones que oyes.

MARÍA: ¿Piensa que _____¹ las gracias por ayudar a mi familia?

JAIME: ¡No! En realidad yo _____² de otras cosas. Y en todo caso, soy yo el que tiene que _____³ disculpas por haber causado tantos problemas. Pero la verdad es que yo no _____⁴ tú... que Ud.... estaba en medio de todo esto.

MARÍA: ¡Aaah! O sea, si yo no hubiera estado en medio, ¿Ud. habría seguido siendo parte de _____⁵ con mi hermano?

Actividad B El episodio

Ahora mira el episodio de nuevo. No te olvides de prestar atención especial a la escena de la **Actividad A** para poder completar el diálogo entre María y Jaime.

Después de ver el episodio

Actividad Intercambio

Ya sabes que hace sólo un día, María no quiso hablar con Jaime. Le dijo a su mamá: «Ese es un nombre que jamás quiero oír de nuevo.» Pero ahora parece que ella perdona a Jaime. ¿A qué crees que se debe este cambio de actitud?

Detrás de la cámara

At the end of the film, Jaime and María reconcile, but not without some difficulty. You already know that María is a very strong-willed person with definite convictions and beliefs. When she found out that Jaime was trying to get Carlos to sell the winery, she took it as a personal offense, thinking that Jaime was using her to get to Carlos. Of course, you know that it was a matter of circumstance that brought Jaime and María together. Or was it? Just as don Paco and doña Isabel conspired to bring Jaime and María together, so too did the forces of nature, as personified by la machi and the mystery man who appears throughout the film. Thus, the story concludes with harmony and balance restored to the Earth and to those that inhabit it.

EPISODIO 9 * UN BRINDIS POR EL FUTURO

73

SOL Y VIENTO: Enfoque cultural

En el **Episodio 9** Jaime tiene un problema con el uso de **tú** y **usted**. Acostumbrado a tratar de **tú** (tratamiento de confianza) a María, le cuesta[a] tratarla de **usted** (tratamiento de distancia) después de que ella puso distancia entre ellos, y él quiere decirle que siente mucho lo que ha pasado. Poco después, tiene que preguntarle a María si pueden volver a tutearse.

El uso de **tú** y **usted** en el mundo hispano no es igual de un país a otro. Claro, hay usos que son casi universales, como ocurre cuando un joven se dirige a una mujer mayor de edad, en cuyo[b] caso es indispensable el uso de **usted**. Lo mismo ocurre al dirigirse a una persona de más respetabilidad que la persona que habla, por ejemplo entre estudiantes y profesores: se da el trato de **usted** al profesor, aunque este llame de **tú** al estudiante.

Al hablar de las variaciones en el uso de **tú** frente a **usted**, es de mencionar que en España, por ejemplo, se utiliza **tú** en casos en los que en México y el Perú predomina el uso de **usted**. En algunos países, los miembros de una familia, incluyendo a los abuelos, se tratan de **usted**, mientras que en otras todos los familiares se tutean. Cuando lees algo en español que se dirige al lector, ya sea un artículo o un anuncio, algunas veces verás que se usa **tú**, y en otras, **usted**.

[a]le... *it's hard for him* [b]*whose*

Para escribir

*

Antes de escribir

Recuerda que la machi comenzó la película narrando una historia, y la voz del narrador nos dice: *She speaks of how the gods seek to keep harmony on the Earth.* Según esta idea, las varias resoluciones, incluyendo las relaciones entre Jaime y María, son manipuladas por los dioses. En esta actividad, vas a escribir sobre la «intervención» de los dioses en las relaciones entre Jaime y María.

Paso 1 Haz una lista de todas las apariciones del «hombre misterioso». ¿Recuerdas quién es? (Es la persona que aparece y desaparece en el **Prólogo**.) Sigue el modelo.

	LUGAR O ESCENA	LO QUE HIZO	CONSECUENCIA
MODELO:	Parque Forestal	Le vendió un papelito de la suerte a Jaime.	Jaime, por estar distraído, chocó con María.

Paso 2 Ahora piensa cómo vas a comenzar tu ensayo. ¿Vas a comenzarlo con una pregunta? ¿con una oración? Compara los siguientes comienzos para estimular tus ideas.

MODELOS: ¿Ha pensado Ud. alguna vez si lo que le pasa se debe solamente al destino, no al libre albedrío (*free will*)? ¿Hay «otro mundo» que nos observa y que asegura (*makes sure*) que todo resulte de una u otra manera? Esta es la premisa de *Sol y viento*.

Desde épocas remotas el hombre siempre ha creído en algo llamado «el destino». Predeterminado por un plan divino o por otra(s) fuerza(s), uno no crea su destino; el destino le toca. Esta es la premisa de *Sol y viento*.

A escribir

Paso 1 Usa las ideas de **Antes de escribir** para escribir un borrador en una hoja de papel aparte.

Paso 2 Mira bien lo que has escrito. ¿Quieres agregar palabras, expresiones u oraciones para hacer la narración más interesante?

ANSWER KEY

Prólogo

Antes de ver el episodio
Actividad B (*Actual answers*) ***María:*** 1. *false* 2. *false* 3. *true* ***Jaime:*** 1. *true* 2. *false* 3. *true* **Actividad C** a
Después de ver el episodio
Actividad A 1. c 2. b 3. b 4. c **Actividad C** *pretty*

Episodio 1

A primera vista
Antes de ver el episodio
Actividad A 1. *false* 2. *true* 3. *true* 4. *true* 5. *true* **Actividad B Paso 2** 1. Para servirlo 2. ¿Qué se le ofrece? 3. ¡Claro que sí!
4. A propósito **Actividad C Paso 1** 1. c 2. b
Después de ver el episodio
Actividad A 1. Sí 2. Hotel Bonaparte 3. Maipo 4. Talavera, Verdejo 5. b 6. a **Actividad C Paso 1** *How much will it be? / Is that okay?* **Paso 2** *Let's go.*

A segunda vista
Antes de ver el episodio
Actividad A 1. la viña 2. con 3. Soy 4. que 5. estoy 6. como 7. Muy bien 8. espero 9. Hasta

Episodio 2

A primera vista
Antes de ver el episodio
Actividad A 1. falso 2. cierto 3. falso 4. cierto 5. falso **Actividad B Paso 2** 1. ¡Qué coincidencia! 2. Ojalá que nos veamos de nuevo 3. ¡Espere! **Actividad C** 1. b 2. a 3. c 4. a
Después de ver el episodio
Actividad A 1. b 2. c 3. c 4. b 5. a 6. b **Actividad C** *I was distracted; (he) was reading*
Actividad D 1. corre 2. vende 3. lee 4. se choca con 5. decide 6. espera 7. hablan 8. necesita

A segunda vista
Antes de ver el episodio
Actividad A 1. Tres 2. Tres 3. trescientos 4. Esa 5. esa 6. esa 7. trescientos 8. estos

Episodio 3

A primera vista
Antes de ver el episodio
Actividad A 1. falso 2. cierto 3. cierto 4. cierto 5. falso **Actividad B Paso 2** 1. f 2. a 3. d 4. e 5. c 6. b **Actividad C** 1. b 2. c 3. b
Después de ver el episodio
Actividad A 1. b 2. a 3. a 4. a 5. a 6. a **Actividad C** Traimaqueo lo puede guiar: lo = a Ud. (Jaime); Yo lo voy a llamar... : lo = a él (Traimaqueo) **Actividad D** 1. conoce 2. toman 3. hablan 4. venta 5. quiere 6. tiene 7. insiste 8. contrato

A segunda vista
Antes de ver el episodio
Actividad A 1. bodega 2. vino 3. vino chileno 4. prefiero 6. importantes 6. oficina

Episodio 4

A primera vista
Antes de ver el episodio
Actividad A 1. Jaime 2. María 3. Mario, Carlos 4. la madre de Carlos, Carlos **Actividad B Paso 2** 1. regalo 2. cepas 3. Nací, me enterrarán 4. se equivocan 5. topacio **Actividad C** b
Después de ver el episodio
Actividad A 1. Traimaqueo. Mario no los acompañó. 2. no 3. No, no le dijo la verdad. 4. para María **Actividad C** 1. *Is that okay with you?* 2. *How much is it? / I'll take it.* **Actividad D** 1. conoce 2. poema 3. pasión 4. madre 5. agradable 6. pueblo mapuche 7. espíritu

A segunda vista
Antes de ver el episodio
Actividad A 1. profesora 2. para 3. lindo 4. tarjeta

Episodio 5

A primera vista
Antes de ver el episodio
Actividad A 1. falso 2. cierto 3. cierto 4. falso 5. falso **Actividad B Paso 2** 1. Los campesinos 2. La Bolsa (de valores) 3. Te encargaste de 4. Brindemos 5. Vamos a tutearnos **Actividad C** 1. b 2. b 3. a
Después de ver el episodio
Actividad A 1. b 2. a 3. Habló con su esposo que ya murió. 4. «gente de la tierra» 5. b 6. b 7. b **Actividad C** 1. no van bien 2. quiere vender 3. no le gusta nada 4. pasan 5. le parece que 6. le cuenta 7. van bien 8. le da

A segunda vista
Antes de ver el episodio
Actividad A 1. quedé 2. pasa 3. pasa 4. conozco 5. tengo 6. murió 7. encargaste 8. estaba 9. tenía

Episodio 6

A primera vista
Antes de ver el episodio
Actividad A 1. cierto 2. falso 3. falso 4. cierto 5. cierto **Actividad B Paso 2** 1. jitomates 2. ¿Qué tal están? 3. ¡Pruébelos!
4. Déme **Actividad C** 1. a 2. b
Después de ver el episodio
Actividad A 1. b 2. a 3. b 4. b 5. b **Actividad C Paso 1** *How fresh/good are . . . ?* **Paso 2** «Aló» / «Diga» **Actividad D** 1. está
preocupada 2. le cae bien 3. lo respeta 4. conoce a 5. está a la venta 6. aeropuerto 7. el amuleto

A segunda vista
Antes de ver el episodio
Actividad A 1. Nos 2. tampoco 3. tierras 4. espere 5. necesaria 6. le dije 7. hermana 8. he visto 9. importa

Episodio 7

A primera vista
Antes de ver el episodio
Actividad A 1. falso 2. cierto 3. cierto 4. cierto 5. falso **Actividad B Paso 2** 1. represa 2. ruedas 3. atraviesa por 4. el repuesto
5. los hechos **Actividad C** 1. b 2. b
Después de ver el episodio
Actividad A 1. c 2. a 3. c 4. a 5. b **Actividad C** 1. se les pinchó 2. repuesto 3. insolación 4. le informó 5. la comunidad
6. sus acciones

A segunda vista
Antes de ver el episodio
Actividad A 1. perdonar 2. A menos que 3. merezca

Episodio 8

A primera vista
Antes de ver el episodio
Actividad A 1. Mario, Jaime 2. doña Isabel, Jaime 3. don Paco, Jaime 4. Jaime, doña Isabel 5. Jaime, don Paco y doña
Isabel. **Actividad B Paso 2** 1. deudas 2. renunciar a 3. engañar 4. invitados 5. fracasar
Actividad C a
Después de ver el episodio
Actividad A 1. b 2. c 3. a 4. c **Actividad C** *Stop!, You should go change* **Actividad D** 1. descubrió 2. engañaba 3. le pidió
4. respondió 5. tenía 6. se lo contó todo 7. le preguntó 8. había hecho 9. lo había perdido 10. le dio

A segunda vista
Antes de ver el episodio
Actividad A 1. ibas 2. engañaste 3. seducirme 4. sabía 5. se conocían 6. has hecho 7. se maneja

Episodio 9

A primera vista

Antes de ver el episodio

Actividad A 1. resentido 2. María se lo dijo. 3. Porque don Paco lo invitó. 4. Ella puede llamar a las autoridades o él puede renunciar a su conexión con la viña y desaparecer. 5. su corazón **Actividad B Paso 2** 1. bienvenidos 2. hacerme cargo 3. humilde 4. A lo mejor **Actividad C** 1. familia 2. sea 3. quiero 4. presentar

Después de ver el episodio

Actividad A 1. Han oído rumores de la venta de «Sol y viento». 2. Que tienen un acuerdo con un distribuidor y van a expandir las exportaciones a Norteamérica. **Actividad C** 1. *What's really going on?* 2. *As long as I still live, nothing will happen to this vineyard or to this land!* 3. *Nothing will be sold here!* **Actividad D** 1. dice 2. por 3. Les 4. se vende 5. Mientras

A segunda vista

Antes de ver el episodio

Actividad A 1. debo darle 2. quería hablar 3. pedir 4. sabía que 5. ese negocio

SPANISH-ENGLISH VOCABULARY

✱

This Spanish-English Vocabulary contains all the words that appear in the film *Sol y viento*.

Gender is indicated except for masculine nouns ending in **-o**, feminine nouns ending in **-a**, and invariable adjectives. Stem changes and spelling changes are indicated for verbs: **dormir (ue, u); llegar (gu).**

Because **ch** and **ll** are no longer considered separate letters, words with **ch** and **ll** are alphabetized as they would be in English. The letter **ñ** follows the letter **n: añadir** follows **anuncio,** for example.

The following abbreviations are used:

adj.	adjective	*m.*	masculine
adv.	adverb	*Mex.*	Mexico
Arg.	Argentina	*n.*	noun
aux.	auxiliary	*neut.*	neuter
conj.	conjunction	*obj.*	object
def. art.	definite article	*p.p.*	past participle
d.o.	direct object	*pl.*	plural
f.	feminine	*poss.*	possessive
fam.	familiar	*prep.*	preposition
form.	formal	*pron.*	pronoun
gram.	grammatical term	*refl.*	reflexive
indef. art.	indefinite article	*s.*	singular
inf.	infinitive	*Sp.*	Spain
inv.	invariable	*sub. pron.*	subject pronoun
i.o.	indirect object	*v.*	verb
irreg.	irregular		

A

a to, at; **a continuación** following; **a la derecha de** to the right of; **a la izquierda de** to the left of; **a la misma hora** at the same time; **a la(s)...** at ... o'clock; **a menos que** unless; **a menudo** often; **a pesar de** *prep.* in spite of, despite; **¿a qué hora?** at what time?; **a solas** alone; **llegar (gu) a tiempo** to arrive on time
abajo below, underneath
abierto/a (*p.p. of* **abrir**) open
abogado/a lawyer
abogar (gu) por to advocate
abordar to board
aborto abortion
abrazar (c) to embrace
abrigo overcoat

abril *m.* April
abrir (*p.p.* **abierto/a**) to open
✓**abrochar(se) (el cinturón)** to fasten (*uno's* seatbelt)
absoluto/a absolute; complete
abstención *f.* abstention
abstracto/a abstract
abuelo/a grandfather, grandmother; *pl.* grandparents
aburrido/a bored; boring
aburrir(se) to bore (oneself)
abusar de to abuse (*someone*)
acá here
acabar to finish; **acabar de** + *inf.* to have just (*done something*)
academia academy
académico/a academic
acampar to camp
✓**acaparado/a** monopolized

✓**acariciar** to caress
acaso: por si acaso just in case
acceder a to consent to
acceso access
accesorio accessory
accidente *m.* accident
acción *f.* action; **Día** (*m.*) **de Acción de Gracias** Thanksgiving; *pl.* stocks
aceite *m.* oil; **aceite de oliva** olive oil
aceptable acceptable
aceptación *f.* acceptance
aceptar to accept
acerca de about
acero steel
acertar (ie) to guess right
ácido acid
✓**aclaración** *f.* clarification

acomodar to settle; to make
comfortable
acompañar to accompany; to go
with
acondicionado: aire (m.)
acondicionado air conditioning
aconsejar to advise
✓acontecimiento event, happening
acostarse (ue) to go to bed
acostumbrarse a to get used to, to
become accustomed to
actitud f. attitude
actividad f. activity
activista m., f. activist
activo/a active
acto act
actor m. actor
actriz f. (pl. actrices) actress
✓actual current; contemporary
actualidad f.: en la actualidad
currently
actuar (actúo) to act
acuario Aquarius
acuático/a aquatic
acuerdo agreement; estar (irreg.) de
acuerdo to agree; ponerse (irreg.)
de acuerdo to come to an
agreement
adaptable adaptable
adaptarse to adapt
adecuado/a appropriate
adelante adv. ahead
además moreover; además de
besides
adentro adv. inside
adicional additional
adiós good-bye
adivinar to guess
adjetivo adjective
administración f. administration;
administración de empresas
business administration (P)
administrador(a) administrator
admirador(a) fan, admirer
admirar to admire
adolescencia adolescence
adolescente m., f. adolescent,
teenager
¿adónde? where (to)?
adoptar to adopt
adoptivo/a adopted

adorar to adore, worship
adquirido/a acquired; síndrome (m.)
de inmunodeficiencia adquirida
(SIDA) Acquired Immune
Deficiency Syndrome (AIDS)
adquisición f. acquisition
aduana s. customs; pasar por la
aduana to go through customs
adulto/a adult; edad (f.) adulta
adulthood
adverbio adverb
advertir (ie, i) (de) to warn (about)
aéreo/a: línea aérea airline
aeróbico aerobic; hacer (irreg.)
ejercicio aeróbico to do aerobics
aeropuerto airport
afán m. desire
afectar to affect
afectuoso/a affectionate
afeitarse to shave
aficionado/a fan; ser (irreg.)
aficionado/a (a) to be a fan (of)
afirmación f. statement
afirmar to affirm
afirmativo/a adj. affirmative
afluencia throng, horde
afortunadamente fortunately, luckily
África Africa
africano/a n., adj. African
afroamericano/a n., adj. African-
American
afuera adv. outside; n. pl. suburbs,
outskirts
agencia agency; agencia de viajes
travel agency
agenda electrónica electronic
organizer, PDA (personal digital
assistant)
agente m., f. agent; agente de
inmobilaria real estate agent;
agente de viajes travel agent
agitado/a agitated, shaken
agosto August
agradable pleasant, nice
agradar to please
agradecer (zc) to thank
agradecido/a thankful
agregar (gu) to add
agrícola adj. m., f. agricultural
agrio/a sour
agrupación f. group

agrupar to group
agua f. (but el agua) water; agua
corriente running water; agua del
grifo tap water; agua potable
drinking water; contaminación (f.)
del agua water pollution; esquiar
(esquío) en el agua to water ski
aguacate m. avocado
aguado/a watered down
aguafiestas m., f. s. party-pooper
aguantar to endure; no aguantar not
to be able to stand, put up with
ahí there
ahora now
ahorrar to save
ahorros pl. savings; cuenta de
ahorros savings account
aimará m. Aimara (language)
aire m. air; aire acondicionado air
conditioning; al aire libre
outdoors; contaminación (f.) del
aire air pollution
aislado/a isolated
ajedrez m. chess
ajeno/a foreign
ajo garlic
al (contraction of a + el) to the; al
aire libre outdoors; al este de to the
east of; al horno baked; al igual que
just like; al lado de beside; al norte
de to the north of; al oeste de to the
west of; al sur de to the south of; al
vapor steamed
alarma m. alarm
alarmante alarming
alberca (Mex.) swimming pool
alcachofa artichoke
alcanzar (c) (una meta) to reach,
achieve (a goal)
alcoba bedroom
alcohol m. alcohol
alcohólico/a adj. alcoholic; bebida
alcohólica alcoholic drink
alegrarse to get, become happy
alegre happy
alegría happiness
alemán m. German (language) (P)
alergia allergy
alérgico/a allergic
alfombra rug; carpet
algo something, some

algodón *m.* cotton
alguien someone
algún, alguno/a some, any
alianza alliance
aliento breath; **mal aliento** bad breath
alimenticio/a nutritional
alimento food item
aliviar to alleviate
allá (way) over there
allí there; over there
almacén *m.* department store
almendrado/a almond-shaped
almohada pillow
almorzar (ue) (c) to eat lunch
almuerzo lunch
alojamiento lodging
alojarse to stay (*in a place*)
alpinismo rock climbing; **practicar (qu) el alpinismo de rocas** to rock climb
alquilar to rent; **se alquila** for rent
alquiler *m.* rent
alrededor de *prep.* around
alternativa *n.* alternative, choice
alterno/a alternating
alto/a tall; high; **en voz alta** aloud; **zapatos de tacón alto** high-heeled shoes
altruista *adj. m., f.* altruistic
altura height
alubia bean
aluminio aluminum; **lata de aluminio** aluminum can
alza rise
amable friendly
amante *m., f.* lover
amar to love
amargo/a bitter
amarillo/a yellow
Amazonas: río Amazonas Amazon River
amazónico/a *adj.* Amazon
ambicioso/a ambitious
ambiente *m.* atmosphere; **medio ambiente** environment
ambigüedad *f.* ambiguity
ambos/as *pl.* both
amenaza threat
americano/a American; **fútbol** (*m.*) **americano** football

amerindio/a *adj.* indigenous to the Americas
amigo/a friend
amistad *f.* friendship
amor *m.* love
amoroso/a affectionate, loving
amortizar (c) una deuda to pay off a debt; **amortizar una hipoteca** to pay off a mortgage
amplio/a ample, broad
amueblado/a furnished
amuleto amulet
analfabetismo illiteracy
análisis *m. inv.* analysis
analista *m., f.* analyst; **analista de sistemas** systems analyst
analítico/a analytical
anaranjado/a orange (*color*)
andar *irreg.* to walk; **andar en bicicleta** to ride a bicycle; **rueda de andar** treadmill
andino/a Andean
anfitrión, anfitriona host, hostess
ángel *m.* angel
anglohablante *m., f.* English speaker; *adj.* English-speaking
angloparlante *m., f.* English speaker
animal *m.* animal
animar to encourage; to animate; to energize
aniversario anniversary
anoche *adv.* last night
anotar to note, take note of
ansioso/a worried, anxious
Antártida Antarctica
ante *prep.* before; faced with; in the presence of
antemano: de antemano ahead of time
anteojos *pl.* glasses (*vision*)
antepasado/a ancestor
antes *adv.* before; **antes de** (*prep.*) + *inf.* before (*doing something*); **antes (de) que** *conj.* before
anticipación *f.:* **con dos horas de anticipación** two hours ahead of time
anticipar to anticipate, foresee
antiguo/a old
antioxidante antioxidizing

antirrobo/a antitheft; **seguro antirrobo** antitheft insurance
antropología anthropology (P)
antropólogo/a anthropologist
anuncio advertisement; announcement; **anuncio publicitario** commercial
añadir to add
año year; **cada año** each year; **¿cuántos años cumples?** how many years old are you (*turning*) (*fam. s.*)?; **cumplir... años** to be . . . old (*on a birthday*); **hace... años** . . . years ago; **tener** (*irreg.*)**... años** to be . . . years old
apagar (gu) to turn off (*light*)
aparato appliance; **aparato doméstico** household appliance; **aparato electrónico** electronic device
aparecer (zc) to appear
aparente apparent
apariencia appearance
apartamento apartment
aparte *adv.* apart; besides; **hoja de papel aparte** separate piece of paper
apasionado/a passionate
apatía apathy
apático/a apathetic
apellido last name; **¿cuál es su apellido?** what's his/her last name? (P); **¿cuál es tu apellido?** what's your (*fam. s.*) last name? (P); **mi apellido es...** my last is . . . (P)
apenas *adv.* hardly; barely
aperitivo appetizer
apetecer (zc) to appeal, be pleasing
aplicarse (qu) to apply oneself
apodarse to be nicknamed
apoyar to support
apoyo support
apreciar to appreciate
aprender to learn
apresurar to rush
aprobar (ue) to approve, pass
apropiado/a appropriate
aprovecharse (de) to take advantage (of)
aproximadamente approximately

apuntar to note, jot down

apunte *m.* note; **tomar apuntes** to take notes

apurado/a hurried, rushed

aquel, aquella *adj.* that (over there); *pron.* that one (over there)

aquello *neut. pron.* that; that thing

aquí here

árabe *n., adj. m., f.* Arab

araña spider

árbol *m.* tree; **árbol genealógico** family tree; **subirse a los árboles** to climb trees

archipiélago archipelago, group of islands

archivo archive, file

área *f.* (*but* **el área**) area

arena sand

argentino/a *n., adj.* Argentine

arma *f.* (*but* **el arma**) **de fuego** firearm

armado/a armed; **fuerzas armadas** armed forces

armario closet

armonía harmony, agreement

arquitecto/a architect

arquitectura architecture; **arquitectura paisajista** landscape architecture

arreglar to fix

arrepentirse (ie, i) (de) to be sorry (about); to regret

arriba *prep.* up

arriesgado/a daring, risk-taking

arrogante arrogant

arroz *m.* rice

arruinar to ruin

arte *m.* (*but* **las artes**) art; *pl.* arts (P)

arterial: presión (*f.*) **arterial** blood pressure

artículo article

artista *m., f.* artist

artístico/a artistic

ascendencia heritage

ascensor *m.* elevator

asegurado/a insured

asesinar to murder

asesor(a) consultant

así thus, so; **así así** so-so, fair; **así que** so (that), therefore

Asia Asia

asiático/a *n., adj.* Asian

asiáticoamericano *n., adj.* Asian-American

asiento chair

asignar to assign

asistente (*m., f.*) **de vuelo** flight attendant

asistir (a) to attend

asociación *f.* association

asociado/a associated; **Estado Libre Associado** Free Associated State, Commonwealth

asociar to associate; to combine

aspecto aspect; appearance

aspiración *f.* aspiration, hope

aspiradora vacuum; **pasar la aspiradora** to vacuum

aspirina aspirin

astronomía astronomy (P)

astrónomo/a astronomer

astuto/a astute, clever

asumir to assume

asunto subject, topic, issue

atacar (qu) to attack

atajo shortcut

atención *f.* attention

atender (ie) to wait on

atentado *n.* attack

atento/a attentive

atlántico/a: océano Atlántico Atlantic Ocean

atleta *m., f.* athlete

atlético/a athletic

atracción *f.* attraction; *pl.* amusements

atractivo/a attractive

atrapado/a trapped

atrasado/a backward

atravesar (ie) to cross; to run through (*river*)

atrevido/a daring

atribuirse (y) todo el mérito to take all the credit

atún *m.* tuna

audiencia audience

auditorio/a auditorium (P)

aumentar to augment, increase

aumento *n.* increase

aun *adv.* even

aún *adv.* still, yet

aunque although

ausencia absence

Australia Australia

auto car

autobús *m.* bus; **parada de autobuses** bus stop

autoconsciente *m., f.* self-conscious

automático/a automatic; **cajero automático** ATM; **contestador** (*m.*) **automático** answering machine

automóvil *m.* automobile; **seguro de automóvil** automobile insurance

autonomía *individual political entity or region* (*Sp.*)

autónomo/a autonomous

autoridad *f.* authority

autorizar (c) to authorize

autostop *m.:* **hacer** (*irreg.*) **autostop** to hitchhike

avance *m.* advance

avanzar (c) to advance

ave *f.* (*but* **el ave**) bird; *pl.* poultry

aventurarse to risk

aventurero/a adventurous

avergonzado/a embarrassed

averiguar (averigüo) to find out

avión *m.* airplane

ayer yesterday

ayuda *n.* help; **pedir (i, i) ayuda** to ask for help

ayudante *m., f.* helper; assistant

ayudar to help

ayuntamiento city (town) hall

azteca *n. m., f.; adj.* Aztec

azúcar *m.* sugar; **cañaveral** (*m.*) **de azúcar** sugar cane field

azul blue

B

bailar to dance; **salir** (*irreg.*) **a bailar** to go dancing

baile *m.* dance

baja *n.* fall (*stocks*)

bajar to go down; **bajar de** to get off; **bajar de peso** to lose weight

bajo *prep.* under

bajo/a *adj.* short (*height*); low; **los Países Bajos** The Netherlands

balcón *m.* balcony

bambalina: tras bambalinas behind the scenes

banana banana

bancario/a *adj.* banking, financial
banco bank
banda band
bandeja tray
bandera flag
bañar to bathe; **bañarse** to take a bath
bañera bathtub
baño bathroom; **con baño (privado)** with a (private) bathroom; **traje** (*m.*) **de baño** bathing suit
bar *m.* bar
barato/a inexpensive, cheap
barbacoa *n.* barbecue
barco ship, boat; **navegar (gu) en barco** to sail
barra bar; **barra de frutas** fruit bar; **barra de granola** granola bar
barrer (el piso) to sweep (the floor)
barrio neighborhood
basar to base, support
base *f.* base, foundation; **a base de** based on
básico/a basic
basquetbol *m.* basketball; **jugar (ue) (gu) al basquetbol** to play basketball
bastante *adv.* somewhat, rather
basura garbage; **sacar (qu) la basura** to take out the trash
basurero landfill
bata robe
bebé *m., f.* baby
beber to drink
bebida *n.* drink; **bebida alcohólica** alcoholic drink
béisbol *m.* baseball
beisbolista *m., f.* baseball player
belleza beauty
bello/a beautiful
beneficios *pl.* benefits
berenjena eggplant
besar to kiss
beso *n.* kiss
biblioteca library (P)
bibliotecario/a librarian
bicicleta bicycle; **andar** (*irreg.*) **en bicicleta** to ride a bicycle
bien *adv.* well; **caerle** (*irreg.*) **bien a alguien** to like someone; **combinar bien** to go well with (*clothing*);

llevarse bien con to get along well with; **manejar bien** to manage well; **¿me queda bien?** does it fit me?; **pasarlo bien** to have a good time; **portarse bien** to behave well; **quedarle bien** to fit well
bienes *m. pl.*: **bienes fabricados** manufactured goods; **bienes raíces** real estate
bienestar *m.* well-being
bilingüe bilingual
bilingüismo bilingualism
billar *m. s.* pool, billiards
billete *m.* ticket (*Sp.*)
biodegradable: producto biodegradable biodegradable product
biografía biography
biología biology (P)
biólogo/a biologist
bistec *m.* steak
blanco/a white; **vino blanco** white wine
blando/a soft
blindar to shield
blusa blouse
boca mouth
bocacalle *f.* intersection
boda wedding; **padrino de boda** groomsman
bodega wine cellar
bolero love song
boleto ticket
bolígrafo pen
boliviano/a *n., adj.* Bolivian
bolsa purse; **Bolsa de valores** stock market
bolso pocketbook; handbag
bonito/a pretty
bono voucher
borrador *m.* eraser (P)
bosque *m.* **(lluvioso)** (rain)forest
botana (*Mex.*) appetizer
botas *pl.* boots
botella bottle; **botella de plástico** plastic bottle; **botella de vidrio** glass bottle
botón *m.* button
botones *m. inv.* bellhop
Brasil *m.* Brazil
brasileño/a Brazilian

bravo/a wild
brazo arm
brécol *m.* broccoli
bretaña: Gran Bretaña Great Britain
breve *adj.* brief
brillar to shine
brindar to toast
brindis *m.* toast
británico/a *adj.* British
bróculi *m.* broccoli
bruto/a: producto nacional bruto gross national product
bucear to snorkel
buen, bueno/a good; **buen provecho** enjoy your meal; **buenas noches** good night (P); **buenas tardes** good afternoon/evening (P); **buenos días** good morning (P); **es buena idea** it's a good idea; **estar** (*irreg.*) **a buen precio** it's a good price; **estar** (*irreg.*) **en buena forma** to be in good shape; **hace buen tiempo** it's good weather
bufanda scarf
burlador(a) *adj.* seducer
burlarse de otros to make fun of others
buscar (qu) to look for; **estoy buscando...** I'm looking for . . .
búsqueda *n.* search; **hacer** (*irreg.*) **una búsqueda** to do a search

C

caballero gentleman
caballo horse; **montar a caballo** to go horseback riding
cabello hair
cabeza head; **dolor** (*m.*) **de cabeza** headache
cabezón(a) headstrong
cacahuete *m.* peanut; **mantequilla de cacahuete** peanut butter
cacao cocoa
cacique *m.* chief (*of a tribe*)
cada *inv.* each; **cada año** each year; **cada día** every day; **cada mes** each month; **cada uno** each one; **cada vez** each time; **cada vez más** more and more
cadena (TV) network

caer(se) *irreg.* to fall; **caerle bien/mal a alguien** to (dis)like someone; **¿en qué día (mes) cae… ?** what day (month) is . . . ?

café *m.* **(descafeinado)** (decaffeinated) coffee; **café con leche** coffee with milk; **charlar en un café** to chat in a cafe; **tomar café** to drink coffee

cafetera coffeepot

cafetería cafeteria (P)

caída *n.* drop

caja box; cashier's station, checkout counter; **caja de cartón** cardboard box

cajero/a teller; **cajero automático** ATM

cajón *m.* large box

calcetines *m. pl.* socks

calculadora calculator

calcular to calculate

cálculo calculus

calendario calendar

calidad *f.* quality

caliente hot; **chocolate** (*m.*) **caliente** hot chocolate; **té** (*m.*) **caliente** hot tea

callar to silence someone; *refl.* to shut up

calle *f.* street

calmado/a calm

calmante *m.* tranquilizer

calor *m.* heat; **hace (mucho) calor** it's (very) hot

caloría calorie; **quemar calorías** to burn calories

calvo/a bald

calzar (c): ¿qué número calza? what size shoe do you (*form. s.*) wear?

cama bed; **cama matrimonial** queen bed; **cama sencilla** twin bed; **hacer** (*irreg.*) **la cama** to make the bed

cámara digital digital camera

camarero/a waiter, waitress

camarones *m. pl.* shrimp

cambiar (por) to change, exchange (for); **cambiar de canal** to change channels

cambio change; **en cambio** on the other hand

caminar to walk

camino road; **camino a** on the way to

camión *m.* truck; bus (*Mex.*)

camisa shirt

camiseta T-shirt

campanario bell tower

campaña campaign

campeonato championship

campesino/a peasant

camping: hacer (*irreg.*) **camping** to go camping

campo country(side); field (*of work*); **¿cuál es tu campo?** what's your major? (P)

canadiense *n., adj.* Canadian

canal *m.* canal; **cambiar de canal** to change channels; **canal de televisión** television channel

canario canary

cancelar to cancel

cancha (de tenis) (tennis) court

canción *f.* song

candidato/a candidate

canoa canoe; **remar en canoa** to go canoeing

canoso/a: pelo canoso gray hair

cansado/a tired

cansarse to tire

cantante *m., f.* singer

cantar to sing

cantidad *f.* quantity

cañaveral (*m.*) **de azúcar** sugar cane field

caótico/a chaotic

capa de ozono ozone layer

capilla chapel

cápita: renta per cápita per capita income

capital *f.* capital (*city*)

capitán *m.* captain

captar to grasp

cara *n.* face

característica characteristic

caracterizar (c) to characterize

carbohidrato carbohydrate

cardíaco/a: infarto cardíaco heart attack

cardiopatía cardiopathy

cargar (gu) to charge

cargo: hacerse (*irreg.*) **cargo de** to take charge of (*something*)

Caribe *m.* Caribbean (Sea)

caribeño/a *n., adj.* of or from the Caribbean

caries *f. inv.* cavity

cariño affection; **tenerle** (*irreg.*) **cariño a alguien** to be fond of someone

cariñoso/a affectionate

carnaval *m.* carnival; **Martes** (*m.*) **de Carnaval** Mardi Gras

carne *f.* meat; **carne de res** beef

carnero *n.* ram

carnicería butcher's shop

caro/a expensive

carrera major; career; **¿qué carrera haces?** what's your (*fam. s.*) major? (P)

carretera highway

carro *m.* car

carta letter

cartel *m.* poster

cartelera billboard

cartera wallet

cartón *m.* cardboard; **caja de cartón** cardboard box

casa house; **casa particular** private residence; **casa privada** private residence; **compañero/a de casa** housemate; **limpiar la casa (entera)** to clean the (whole) house; **regresar a casa** to go home

casado/a married

casamentero/a matchmaker

casarse (con) to marry, get married

casi almost; **casi nunca** almost never; **casi siempre** almost always

caso case; **en caso de que** *conj.* in case

castaño/a brown

castellano *n.* Spanish (*language*)

castellano/a *adj.* Castilian

castigar (gu) to punish

castillo castle

casualidad *f.* chance; coincidence

catalán/catalana *n., adj.* Catalonian

catálogo *n.* catalog

cataratas *pl.* waterfall

catástrofe *f.* catastrophe

catedral *f.* cathedral

categoría category; class

catolicismo Catholicism

católico/a *n., adj.* Catholic
catorce fourteen
causa cause; **a causa de** because of
causar to cause
cautela caution
cazuela casserole
CD: reproductor (*m.*) **de CD** CD player
cebolla onion
celebración *f.* celebration
celebrar to celebrate
célebre famous
celos *pl.* jealousy; **tener** (*irreg.*)
  celos to be jealous
celoso/a jealous; **estar** (*irreg.*)
  celoso/a to be jealous
celular: (teléfono) celular cell phone
cena dinner
cenar to eat/have (for) dinner; **cenar
  en un restaurante elegante** to eat
  in a fancy restaurant
cenizas *pl.* ashes
censurar to judge
centígrado/a centigrade
centro downtown; **centro comercial**
  shopping center, mall; **centro
  estudiantil** student center/union
Centroamérica Central America
centroamericano/a *n., adj.* of or from
  Central America
cepas *pl.* vine stocks
cepillo brush
cerca de *prep.* close to
cerdo pork; **chuleta de cerdo** pork
  chop
cereal (cocido) (cooked) cereal
cerebral cerebral
cerebro brain
ceremonia ceremony
cero zero
cerrar (ie) to close
cerveza beer; **tomar cerveza** to drink
  beer
chamán *m.* shaman
champiñones *m. pl.* mushrooms
champú *m.* shampoo
chapulín *m.* grasshopper
chaqueta jacket
charadas: juego de charadas
  charades
charlar to chat; **charlar en un café** to
  chat in a cafe

chatarro/a: comida chatarra junk
  food
chau ciao
cheque *m.* check; **cheque de viajero**
  traveler's check
chequear to check
chícharo pea
chico/a *n. m., f.* boy, girl (P); *adj.*
  small
chileno/a *n., adj.* Chilean
chimpancé *m.* chimpanzee
chisme *m.* gossip; **contar (ue)
  chismes** to gossip
chismear to gossip
chismoso/a gossipy
chiste *m.* joke
chocante shocking
chocar (qu) to run into
chocolate *m.* chocolate; **chocolate
  caliente** hot chocolate
chubasco rainstorm
chuleta de cerdo pork chop
cibercafé *m.* cybercafe
ciclismo cycling; **hacer** (*irreg.*)
  ciclismo estacionario to ride a
  stationary bike
cielo sky; heaven
cien, ciento one hundred; **ciento
  uno/a; por ciento** percent
cien mil one hundred thousand
ciencia science; **ciencias naturales**
  natural sciences (P); **ciencias
  políticas** political science (P);
  ciencias sociales social sciences
  (P)
científico/a scientist; *adj.* scientific
cierto/a certain; true
cifra number, figure
cigarillo cigarette
cima top
cinco five
cincuenta fifty
cine *m.* movie theater; the movies; **ir**
  (*irreg.*) **al cine** to go to the movies
cinta cassette
cintura waist
cinturón *m.* belt; **abrocharse el
  cinturón** to fasten one's seatbelt
circulación *f.* circulation; traffic
círculo circle
circunstancia circumstance

cirugía surgery
cirujano/a surgeon
cita appointment; date
ciudad *f.* city
ciudadano/a citizen
cívico/a civic; **responsabilidad** (*f.*)
  cívica civic duty; **reunión** (*f.*)
  cívica town meeting
civil: ingeniería civil civil
  engineering (P); **ingeniero/a civil**
  civil engineer
civilización *f.* civilization
clarificación *f.* clarification
claro/a clear; light
clase *f.* class (P); **clase media** middle
  class; **clase turística** tourist class;
  compañero/a de clase classmate;
  primera clase first class; **¿qué
  clases tienes este
  semestre/trimestre?** what classes
  do you (*fam. s.*) have this
  semester/quarter? (P); **sala de
  clase** classroom (P); **tengo una
  clase de…** I have a(n) … class (P);
  tomar una clase to take a class
clasificación *f.* classification
clasificar (qu) to classify
clave *f.* key
clic: hacer (*irreg.*) **clic** to click
cliente *m., f.* customer
clima *m.* climate
clínica clinic
coágulo clot
cobrar to charge (*a fee*)
cocido/a cooked; **cereal** (*m.*) **cocido**
  cooked cereal
coche *m.* car
cocina kitchen; cooking
cocinar to cook
cocinero/a cook
codiciado/a coveted
código code
codo elbow
coexistir to coexist
cognado cognate
coincidencia coincidence
coincidir to coincide
cola tail (*of an animal*); line (*of
  people*); **hacer** (*irreg.*) **cola** to wait
  (stand) in line
colaborar to collaborate

colección *f.* collection

coleccionar to collect; **coleccionar estampillas** to collect stamps; **coleccionar monedas** to collect coins

colega *m., f.* colleague

colegio high school

colesterol *m.* cholesterol

colgar (ue) (gu) to hang

coliflor *f.* cauliflower

colina hill

colocar (qu) to place

colombiano/a *n., adj.* Colombian

colonia colony

colonizar (c) to colonize

color *m.* color

colorear to color

columna column

comandante commander

combatir to fight

combinación *f.* combination

combinar to combine; **combinar bien** to go well with (*clothing*)

combustibles (*m.*) **fósiles** fossil fuels

comedia comedy

comedor *m.* dining room

comentar to comment, make comments on; to discuss

comentario comment; remark; *pl.* commentaries

comenzar (ie) (c) to begin

comer to eat; **dar** (*irreg.*) **de comer** to feed

comercial: centro comercial shopping center, mall

comercio business (P); **Tratado de Libre Comercio (TLC)** North American Free Trade Agreement (NAFTA)

comestible *m.* food item

cometer to commit

cómico/a funny, comical; **tiras cómicas** comics

comida food; meal; **comida chatarra** junk food; **comida rápida** fast food

comienzo *n.* beginning

comisión *f.* commission

como as, like; **tan pronto como** as soon as

¿cómo? how; ¿cómo es? what is he/she/it like? what are you (*form. s.*) like?; ¿cómo se llama (él/ella)? what's his/her name? (P); ¿cómo se llega a... ? how do you get to . . . ?; ¿cómo te llamas? what's your (*fam. s.*) name? (P)

cómoda dresser, chest of drawers

comodidades *f. pl.* amenities, conveniences

cómodo/a comfortable

compañero/a companion; **compañero/a de casa** housemate; **compañero/a de clase** classmate; **compañero/a de cuarto** roommate

compañía company; **servir (i, i) de compañía** to give, keep company

comparación *f.* comparison

comparar to compare

compartir to share

compasión *f.* compassion

competición *f.* competition

competidor(a) competitive

competir (i, i) to compete

complemento *gram.* pronoun

completar to complete

completo/a complete; **pensión (*f.*) completa** room and all meals

comportamiento behavior

comportarse to behave, act

composición *f.* composition

comprar to buy; **comprar recuerdos** to buy souvenirs

compras purchases; **de compras** shopping

comprender to understand; to encompass

comprensivo/a understanding

comprometer to compromise; to involve; **comprometerse (con)** to get engaged (to)

compuesto/a *adj.* compound

compulsivo/a compulsive

computación *f.* computer science

computadora computer (P); **computadora portátil** laptop computer

común *adj.* common

comunicación *f.* communication; **medios (*pl.*) de communication** media; *pl.* communications (P)

comunidad *f.* community

con with (P); **con baño privado** with a private bathroom; **con frecuencia** frequently; **con tal (de) que** provided (that)

concentración *f.* concentration

concentrar to concentrate; to focus; **concentrarse en** to concentrate in, be concentrated in

concepto concept, idea

concierto concert; ir (*irreg.*) **a un concierto** to go to a concert

conclusión *f.* conclusion

concordancia *gram.* agreement

concurso contest; game show

condición *f.* condition

condicional *m. gram.* conditional

condimentos condiments

condominio condominium

conducir *irreg.* to drive; **sacar (qu) la licencia de conducir** to get a driver's license

conducta conduct, behavior

conductor(a) driver

conectar to connect

conejo rabbit

conexión *f.* connection

confesar (ie) to confess

confiable trustworthy

confiado/a trusting

confianza trust

confiar (confío) (en) to trust (in)

confidente confident

confirmar to confirm

conflicto conflict; **resolver (ue) conflictos** to resolve conflicts

confrontación *f.* confrontation

confrontar to confront

confundido/a confused

confundir to confuse; *refl.* to get confused

confusión *f.* confusion

confuso/a confusing

congelación *n. f.* freezing

congelado/a frozen

congelador *m.* freezer

congelar to freeze; **congelarse** to freeze up (*the screen*)

conjunto outfit; entirety

conmigo with me

conocer (zc) to know, be familiar with (*someone, something*)
conocido/a acquaintance
conocimiento awareness; *pl.* knowledge
conquista conquest
conquistar to conquer; to succeed in seducing someone
consecuencia consequence
conseguir (i, i) (g) to get, obtain; **conseguir** + *inf.* to succeed in (*doing something*)
consejo piece of advice; *pl.* advice
consenso consent
consentido *n.* whim, fancy
consentido/a indulged, spoiled
conservación *f.* conservation
conservador(a) conservative
conservar to preserve, conserve
consideración *f.* consideration
considerar to consider
consistir en to consist of
consolar (ue) to console
constante *adj.* constant
constitución *f.* constitution
constituir (y) to constitute
construir (y) to build
consultar to consult
consultorio doctor's office
consumidor(a) *n.* consumer
consumir to eat; to use up
consumo consumption
contabilidad *f.* accounting (P)
contacto contact
contador(a) accountant
contaminación *f.* pollution; **contaminación del agua** water pollution; **contaminación del aire** air pollution
contaminar to contaminate
contar (ue) to count; to tell; **contar chismes** to gossip
contener (*like* tener) to contain
contenido *s.* contents
contento/a happy
contestador (*m.*) automático answering machine
contestar to answer
contexto context
contigo *fam. s.* with you
continente *m.* continent

continuación *f.* continuation; **a continuación** following
continuar (continúo) to continue
continuo/a continuous
contra: en contra opposed
contraer (*like* traer) to contract
contrario *n.* opposite, contrary
contraseña password
contraste *m.* contrast
contratar to hire
contrato lease
contribución *f.* contribution
contribuir (y) to contribute
controlar to control; to inspect
controvertido/a controversial
convencer (z) to convince
conversación *f.* conversation
convertir (ie, i) to change; **convertirse en** to turn into
coordinación *f.* coordination
copa (wine) glass
copiar to copy
coqueto/a flirtatious
corazón *m.* heart
corbata necktie
cordillera mountain range
correcto/a correct
corregir (i, i) (j) to correct
correo mail; post office; **correo electrónico** e-mail
correr to run
correspondencia correspondence
corresponder to correspond
correspondiente *adj.* corresponding
corriente *n. f.* current; *adj.* current, present; **agua** (*f.* [*but* **el agua**]) **corriente** running water; **cuenta corriente** checking account; **estar** (*irreg.*) **al corriente** to be caught up (*with current events*)
corrupción *f.* corruption
cortar(se) to cut (oneself)
cortés courteous, polite
corto/a short (*except height*); **de corto plazo** short term; **pantalones** (*m. pl.*) **cortos** shorts
cosa thing; **poner** (*irreg.*) **las cosas en orden** to put things in order
cosecha harvest
coser to sew

cosmético/a: cirugía cosmética cosmetic (plastic) surgery
cosmopolita *adj. m., f.* cosmopolitan
costa coast
costar (ue) to cost
costilla rib
costo cost, price
costumbre *f.* custom
cotidiano/a daily
creador(a) creative
crear to create
creativo/a creative
crecer (zc) to grow
creciente *adj.* growing
crédito credit; **tarjeta de crédito** credit card
creencia belief
creer (y) (que) to believe (that); **creo que le queda un poco grande** I think it's a bit big on you
crema cream; **queso de crema** cream cheese
crianza upbringing
crimen *m.* crime; **crimen violento** violent crime
crisis *f.* crisis
cristiano/a *n., adj.* Christian
criticar (qu) to criticize
crítico/a critic
cronológico/a chronological
crucero cruise ship
crudo/a raw
cruel cruel
cruzar (c) to cross
cuaderno notebook
cuadra (city) block
cuadrado/a squared; **metros cuadrados** square meters; **pies** (*m.*) **cuadrados** square feet
cuadro painting; statistical chart; **de cuadros** plaid
cual: tal cual just as
¿cuál(es)? what? which?; **¿cuál es su apellido?** what's his/her last name? (P); **¿cuál es su talla?** what size do you (*form. s.*) wear?; **¿cuál es tu apellido** what's your (*fam. s.*) last name? (P); **¿cuál es tu campo?** what's your major? (P)
cualquier(a) any

cuando when(ever); **de vez en cuando** once in a while

¿cuándo? when?

cuanto: en cuanto as soon as; **en cuanto a** with regard to; **en unos cuantos días** in a few days

cuánto *pron.* **¿a cuánto sale?** how much is it?; **¿cuánto hay de aquí a...** how far is it from here to...?

¿cuántos/as? how many?; **¿cuántos años cumples?** how many years old are you (*turning*) (*fam. s.*)?; **¿cuántos años tiene...?** how old is...?; **¿cuántos años tienes?** how old are you (*fam. s.*)?

cuarenta forty

cuarto *n.* quarter (*of an hour*); fourth; room; **compañero/a de cuarto** roommate; **menos cuarto** a quarter to (*hour*); **servicio de cuarto** room service; **y cuarto** a quarter past (*hour*)

cuarto/a fourth

cuatro four

cuatrocientos/as four hundred

cuatrocientos/as mil four hundred thousand

cubano/a *n., adj.* Cuban

cubierto/a (*p.p. of* **cubrir**) covered

cubiertos *pl.* silverware

cubrir (*p.p.* **cubierto/a**) to cover

cuchara spoon

cuchillo knife

cuello neck

cuenta bill; check; **cuenta corriente** checking account; **cuenta de ahorros** savings account; **darse** (*irreg.*) **cuenta de** to realize

cuento story

cuerda cord; **saltar la cuerda** to jump rope

cuerno horn; **ponerle** (*irreg.*) **los cuernos (a alguien)** to be unfaithful to (some one)

cuero leather

cuerpo body; **partes** (*f. pl.*) **del cuerpo** parts of the body

cuestión *f.* question

cuidado care

cuidar (de) to take care (of)

culpa fault; **echar(le) la culpa (a alguien)** to blame (someone)

culto devotion (*to a god or belief*)

cultura culture

cumpleaños *m. inv.* birthday

cumplido compliment

cumplir (con) to fulfill, carry out; **¿cuántos años cumples?** how many years old are you (*turning*) (*fam. s.*)?; **cumplir... años** to be... old (*on a birthday*); **cumplir las promesas** to keep one's word

cuñado/a brother-in-law, sister-in-law; *pl.* siblings-in-law

curandero/a healer

curar to cure

cursi tacky; cheesy

cursivo/a: letra (*s.*) **cursiva** italics

curso course

cuy *m.* guinea pig

cuyo/a/os/as whose

D

dama lady; **dama de honor** bridesmaid

dañar to hurt, harm

dañino/a harmful

daño damage, hurt

dar *irreg.* to give; **dar de comer** to feed; **dar la vuelta a** to go around (*something*); **dar las gracias** to thank; **dar un paseo** to take a walk; **dar una fiesta** to throw a party; **darle escalofríos a alguien** to give someone chills; **darle rabia (a alguien)** to make (someone) angry; **darse cuenta de** to realize; **darse la mano** to shake hands

dato piece of information; *pl.* data, facts

de *prep.* of (P); from (P); **de compras** shopping; **de corto/largo plazo** short/long term; **de cuadros** plaid; **¿de dónde eres?** where are you (*fam. s.*) from? (P); **de estatura mediana** of medium height: **de ida** one-way; **de ida y vuelta** round-trip; **de la mañana** in the morning (A.M.); **de la noche** in the evening (night) (P.M.); **de la tarde** in the afternoon; **de las... hasta las...** from... (*hour*) to (*hour*); **de lunares** polka-dotted; **¿de qué tamaño es...?** what size is...?; **de rayas** striped; **de repente** suddenly; **de venta** for sale; **de vez en cuando** once in a while; **es de...** it's made of...; **soy de...** I'm from... (P)

debajo de under, below

deber *n. m.* duty

deber + *inf.* ought to, should (*do something*); to owe

debido a due to

débil weak

década decade

decidido/a decisive

decidir to decide

decir *irreg.* (*p.p.* **dicho/a**) to say

decisión *f.* decision

declaración *f.* statement

declarar to declare

dedicación *f.* dedication

dedicarse (qu) a to dedicate oneself to

dedo finger; **dedo del pie** toe

deducción *f.* deduction

deducir (*like* **conducir**) to deduct; to infer

defecto defect

defender (ie) to defend

defensor(a) *n.* defender; *adj.* defensive

definición *f.* definition

definir to define

definitivo/a definitive

deforestación *f.* deforestation

degustar vinos to go wine tasting

dejar to leave; **dejar de** + *inf.* to stop (*doing something*); **dejar en paz** to leave alone; **dejar perplejo/a (a alguien)** to leave (someone) perplexed; **dejar (una) propina** to leave a tip

del (*contraction of* **de** + **el**) of/from the

delante de in front of

delgado/a thin

delicado/a delicate

delicioso/a delicious

demandar to demand

demás: los/las demás others; **dirigir (j) a los demás** to lead others

demasiado *adv.* too, too much

demasiado/a *adj.* too much; *pl.* too many

democracia democracy

democrático/a democratic

demostrar (ue) to demonstrate; to show

demostrativo/a demonstrative

denotar to denote; to indicate

densidad *f.* density

denso/a heavy

dentista *m., f.* dentist

dentro (de) in, within, inside; **dentro de poco** in a little while; **por dentro** within, (on the) inside

depender de to depend on

dependiente/a salesperson

deporte *m.* sport; **practicar (qu) un deporte** to practice a sport

deportivo/a *adj.* sport; **programa** (*m.*) **deportivo** sports show

depositar to deposit

depresión *f.* **(económica)** (economic) depression

deprimido/a depressed

deprimir(se) to depress, become depressed

derecha *n.* right-hand side; **a la derecha (de)** to the right (of); **doblar a la derecha** to turn right

derecho *n.* right (*legal*); law; **derechos humanos** human rights; **seguir (i, i) (g) derecho** to continue straight ahead

derramar to spill

derrocar (qu) to defeat

derrochador(a) wasteful

derrotar to defeat

desafío *n.* challenge

desafortunadamente unfortunately

desagradable unpleasant

desahogarse (gu) con to take it out on

desarrollado/a developed; **país** (*m.*) **desarrollado** developed country

desarrollar to develop

desarrollo (sustenable) (sustainable) development; **país** (*m.*) **en vías de desarrollo** developing country

desastre *m.* **(natural)** (natural) disaster

desastroso/a desastrous

desaventajado/a disadvantaged

desayunar to eat/have (for) breakfast

desayuno breakfast

descafeinado/a decaffeinated; **café** (*m.*) **descafeinado** decaffeinated coffee

descansar to rest

descapotable convertible

descargar (gu) to download

descendiente *m., f.* descendant

descomponer (*like* **poner**) decompose

desconectar to unplug, disconnect

desconfiado/a untrusting

desconocido/a unknown

describir (*p.p.* **descrito/a**) to describe

descripción *f.* description

descubierto/a (*p.p. of* **descubrir**) discovered

descubrimiento discovery

descuento discount

descuidar to neglect

desde *prep.* from; **desde la(s)... hasta la(s)...** from . . . until . . . (*time*)

desear to want, desire

desechable disposable; **producto desechable** disposable product

desechos *pl.* wastes

desempleo unemployment; **tasa de desempleo** unemployment rate

deseo *n.* wish, desire

desierto desert

desilusionado/a disillusioned

desleal disloyal

desobedecer (zc) to disobey

despacio/a slow

despedirse (i, i) to say good-bye

despegar (gu) to take off (*plane*)

despejado/a clear; **está despejado** it's clear (*weather*)

desperdiciar to waste

desperdicios *pl.* waste

despertador *m.* alarm clock

despertarse (ie) to wake up

despreciar to despise

después *adv.* after; **después de** *prep.* after; **después (de) que** *conj.* after

destacado/a outstanding

destacar (qu) to stand out

destino destination; destiny, fate

destrucción *f.* destruction

detalle *m.* detail

detallista *adj. m., f.* detail-oriented

detergente *m.* detergent

determinar to determine

detestar to detest

detrás de *adv.* behind

deuda debt; **amortizar (c) una deuda** to pay off a debt

devoción *f.* devotion

devolver (ue) (*p.p.* **devuelto/a**) to return (*something*)

devoto/a devout

devuelto/a (*p.p. of* **devolver**) returned

día *m.* day; **buenos días** good morning (P); **cada día** every day; **Día de Acción de Gracias** Thanksgiving; **Día de la Madre (del Padre)** Mother's (Father's) Day; **Día de los Enamorados** St. Valentine's Day; **Día de los Reyes Magos** Epiphany (January 6), Day of the Magi; **Día de San Patricio** St. Patrick's Day; **Día de San Valentín** St. Valentine's Day; **día del santo** saint's day; **Día del Trabajo** Labor Day; **día festivo** holiday; **¿en qué día cae... ?** what day is . . . ?; **hoy en día** nowadays; **¿qué día es hoy?** what day is it today?; **todos los días** every day

diabetes *f.* diabetes

dialecto dialect

diálogo dialogue

diario *m.* newspaper

diario/a *adj.* daily

dibujar to draw

dibujo drawing

diccionario dictionary

dicho/a (*p.p. of* **decir**) said

diciembre *m.* December

dictador(a) dictator

dictadura dictatorship

diecinueve nineteen

dieciocho eighteen

dieciséis sixteen

diecisiete seventeen

diente *m.* tooth; **lavarse los dientes** to brush one's teeth

dieta *n.* diet

dietético/a: refresco dietético diet soft drink

diez ten

diez mil ten thousand

diferencia difference; **a diferencia de** unlike

diferenciar (de) to be different (from)

diferente (de) different (from/than)

difícil difficult

dificultad *f.* difficulty

difundirse to diffuse, spread

digestivo/a digestive

digital: cámara digital digital camera

Dinamarca Denmark

dinamismo dynamism, quality of being dynamic

dinero money; **sacar (qu) dinero** to withdraw money

dinosaurio dinosaur

dios(a) god, goddess

diplomático/a diplomat

dirección *f.* direction; address

directo/a direct; straight; **pensar (ie) de manera directa** to think in a direct (linear) manner; **vuelo directo** direct flight

director(a) director

dirigir (j) to direct; **dirigir a los demás** to lead others; **dirigirse a** to direct oneself toward

disco: disco compacto compact disc; **disco duro** hard drive

discoteca discotheque

discreto/a discreet

discriminación *f.* discrimination

disculpar to excuse

disculpas: pedir (*irreg.*) **disculpas** to apologize

discusión *f.* discussion

discutir to discuss; to argue

diseñador(a) designer; **diseñador(a) de sitios** Web site designer

diseñar to draw; to design

disfrutar to enjoy

disponible available

disposición *f.* disposition

dispositivo device

dispuesto/a ready, willing

disquete *m.* diskette

distancia distance; **mando a distancia** remote control

distante distant; far away

distinción *f.* distinction

distinguir (g) to distinguish

distinto/a different, distinct

distorsionado/a distorted

distorsionar to distort

distraer (*like* **traer**) to distract

distribución *f.* distribution

distrito (federal) (federal) district

diversidad *f.* diversity

diversión *f.*: **ir** (*irreg.*) **a un parque de diversiones** to go to an amusement park

diverso/a diverse

divertido/a fun

divertir (ie, i) to entertain; **divertirse** to enjoy oneself

dividirse to divide

divinidad *f.* divinity, god-like being

divorciado/a divorced

divorciarse to divorce, get divorced

divorcio divorce

doblar to turn; **doblar a la derecha/izquierda** to turn right/left

doble double

doce twelve

doctor(a) doctor

doctorado doctoral degree

documental *m.* documentary

documento document; **guardar documentos** to save documents

dólar *m.* dollar

doler (ue) to hurt, ache

dolor *m.* pain; **dolor de cabeza** headache

doméstico/a domestic; **aparato doméstico** household appliance; **quehaceres** (*m.*) **domésticos** household chores; **violencia doméstica** domestic violence

dominación *f.* domination

dominante dominant

dominar to dominate

domingo Sunday

dominicano/a *n., adj.* of or from the Dominican Republic

dominio *n.* control

don *m.* gift, skill; *title of respect used with a man's first name;* **tener** (*irreg.*) **don de gentes** to have a way with people

¿dónde? where?; **¿de dónde eres?** where are you (*fam. s.*) from? (P);

doña *title of respect used with a woman's first name*

dormir (ue, u) to sleep; **dormirse** to fall asleep

dormitorio bedroom

dos two

dos mil two thousand

dos millones two million

doscientos/as two hundred

doscientos mil two hundred thousand

drama *m.* drama

drástico/a drastic

droga drug

drogadicción *f.* drug addiction

ducha shower

ducharse to shower, take a shower

duda doubt; **sin duda** without a doubt

dudar to doubt

dudoso/a doubtful

dueño/a owner

dulce *adj.* sweet; *n. pl.* candy; **pan** (*m.*) **dulce** sweet bread (*Mex.*)

duración *f.* duration

durante during

durar to last

durmiente: la Bella Durmiente Sleeping Beauty

duro/a hard; firm; **disco duro** hard drive

DVD: reproductor (*m.*) **de DVD** DVD player; **sacar (qu) un DVD** to rent a DVD

E

e and (*used instead of* **y** *before words beginning with* **i** *or* **hi**)

echar to throw out; **echar (le) la culpa (a alguien)** to blame (someone); **echar un vistazo** to look over; **echar una siesta** to take a nap

ecología ecology

ecológico/a ecological

economía economy; *s.* economics (P)

económico/a economic; **depresión** (*f.*) **económica** economic depression; **nivel económico** economic level

ecoturismo ecotourism

ecoturista *m., f.* ecotourist

ecoturístico/a *adj.* ecotourist

ecuatoriano/a *n., adj.* Ecuadorean

edad *f.* age; **edad adulta** adulthood

edición *f.* edition

edificio building (P)

educación *f.* education

educar (qu) to educate

educativo/a educational

efectivo: en efectivo cash (money)

efecto effect; **efecto invernadero** greenhouse effect

eficaz (*pl.* **eficaces**) effective

egoísta *adj. m., f.* selfish, egotistical

ejecutivo/a executive

ejemplificar (qu) to exemplify

ejemplo example; **por ejemplo** for example

ejercer (z) to engage in

ejercicio exercise; **hacer** (*irreg.*) **ejercicio** to exercise; **hacer** (*irreg.*) **ejercicio aeróbico** to do aerobics

ejército army

el *def. art. m.* the (P); **el/la mayor** the oldest; **el/la menor** the youngest

él *sub. pron.* he (P); *obj. of prep.* him

elección *f.* election

electricidad *f.* electricity

eléctrico/a electric; **ingeniería eléctrica** electrical engineering (P); **ingeniero/a eléctrico/a** electrical engineer

electrónico/a electronic; **agenda electrónica** electronic organizer, PDA (personal digital assistant); **aparato electrónico** electronic device; **correo electrónico** e-mail

elegante elegant; **cenar en un restaurante elegante** to eat in a fancy restaurant

elegir (i, i) (j) to choose; to elect

elemento element

elevar to elevate, raise

eliminar to eliminate

ella *sub. pron.* she (P); *obj of prep.* her

ellos/as *sub. pron.* they (P); *obj. of prep.* them

embargo: sin embargo *conj.* however

emborracharse to get drunk

emergencia emergency

emocionado/a moved

emocional emotional

emocionante exciting

empanada turnover pie or pastry

emparejar to match

emperador(a) emperor, empress

empezar (ie) (c) to begin; **empezar a** + *inf.* to begin to (*do something*)

empleado/a employee

emplear to use

empleo job; **anuncio de empleo** job ad

empresa company; **administración** (*f.*) **de empresas** business administration (P)

empresarial of or related to business

en in; **en cambio** on the other hand; **en caso de que** in case; **en cuanto** as soon as; **en cuanto a** with regard to; **en punto** on the dot (*time*); **¿en qué día/mes cae... ?** what day/month is . . . ?; **¿en qué puedo servirle?** how may I help you?; **en unos cuantos días** in a few days

enamorado/a (de) in love (with); **Día** (*m.*) **de los Enamorados** St. Valentine's Day

enamorarse (de) to fall in love (with)

encantado/a nice to meet you

encantador(a) delightful, charming

encantar to love; **encantarle** to charm, delight (*someone*); to love (*thing*)

encargarse (de) to take charge (of)

encender (ie) to turn on

enchufe *m.* connection

encima de on top of

enclave *m.* enclave

encontrar (ue) to find; **encontrarse con** to get together (meet) with

encuentro *n.* get-together; (chance) meeting

encuesta survey

energía energy

enérgico/a energetic

enero January

enfermarse to get sick

enfermedad *f.* sickness; disease

enfermero/a *n.* nurse

enfermo/a *n.* sick person; *adj.* sick; **estar** (*irreg.*) **enfermo/a** to be sick

enfoque *m.* focus

enfrentarse a to face, confront

enfrente de across from; in front of

engañador(a) deceitful

engañar to deceive; to cheat on

engañoso/a deceitful

enlace *m.* link

enlatado/a canned

enojado/a angry

enojarse to get mad

enorme enormous

ensalada salad; **ensalada mixta** tossed salad

enseñanza teaching

enseñar to teach

entender (ie) to understand

enterarse de to find out about

entero/a entire, whole; **limpiar la casa entera** to clean the whole house

enterrar (ie) to bury

entonces then

entrada entrance; ticket

entrante: la semana entrante next week

entrar (en + *place*) to enter (*a place*)

entre between

entregar (gu) to hand in

entrelazar (c) to intertwine

entrenamiento training

entrenar to train

entretanto meanwhile

entretener (*like* **tener**) to entertain

entretenido/a amused, entertained, fun

entretenimiento entertainment, amusement

entrevista interview; **programa** (*m.*) **de entrevistas** talk show
entrevistar to interview
entrometerse to meddle
entrometido/a meddlesome
entusiasmado/a enthusiastic; excited
enviar (envío) to send
envidia envy; **tenerle** (*irreg.*) **envidia (a alguien)** to be envious (of someone)
envidioso/a envious
episodio episode
época era, age
equilibrado/a well-balanced
equipado/a equipped
equipaje *m.* luggage; **facturar el equipaje** to check luggage
equipo team; **trabajar en equipo** to work as a team
equivalente equivalent
equivaler (*like* **valer**) to be equivalent; to be equal
equivocarse (qu) to be mistaken
error *m.* error, mistake
erupción *f.* eruption
escala scale; ladder; layover; **hacer** (*irreg.*) **escala** to make a stopover
escalada: practicar (qu) la escalada to rappel
escalar montañas to go mountain climbing
escalofríos *pl.* chills; **darle** (*irreg.*) **escalofríos a alguien** to give someone chills
escandaloso/a scandalous
escapar (de) to escape (from)
escasez (*pl.* **escaseces**) *f.* scarcity
escena scene
esclavo/a slave
escoba broom
escoger (j) to choose
escoliosis *f.* scoliosis
esconder to hide
escondite (*m.*): **jugar (ue) (gu) al escondite** to play hide and seek
escorpión *m.* scorpion
escribir (*p.p.* **escrito/a**) to write
escrito/a (*p.p. of* **escribir**) written
escritor(a) writer
escritorio desk (P)

escuchar to listen (to)
escuela school; **escuela secundaria** high school
escultor(a) sculptor
escultura sculpture
escurrir to drain
ese/a *adj.* that; *pron.* that (one)
eso *neut. pron.* that
esos/esas *adj.* those; *pron.* those (ones)
espacio space; **respetar el espacio personal** to respect personal space
espaguetis *m. pl.* spaghetti
espalda back (*of a person*); **hablar a espaldas de alguien** to talk behind someone's back
espantoso/a scary
español *n. m.* Spanish (*language*) (P)
español(a) *n.* Spaniard; *adj.* Spanish; **tortilla española** *omelette made of eggs, potatoes, and onions*
espárragos *pl.* asparagus
especial special
especialidad *f.* specialty
especialista specialist
especialización *f.* specialization, major
especie *f. s.* species; **especies en peligro de extinción** endangered species
específico/a specific
espectáculo spectacle, sight; show; **mundo de los espectáculos** entertainment industry; **ver** (*irreg.*) **un espectáculo** to see a show
espejo mirror
espera: sala de espera waiting room
esperanza hope
esperar to hope; to wait for
espinacas *pl.* spinach
espíritu *m.* spirit
esponja sponge
espontáneo/a spontaneous
esposo/a husband, wife; *pl.* married couple
espuma foam
esquiar (esquío) (en el agua) to (water) ski
esquina corner (*street*)
estable *adj.* stable

establecer (zc) to establish
establecimiento establishment
estación *f.* season; station; **estación del tren** train station
estacionar to park
estacionario stationary; **hacer** (*irreg.*) **ciclismo estacionario** to ride a stationary bike
estadio stadium
estado *n.* state; condition; **estado físico** physical condition; **Estado Libre Asociado** Free Associated State, Commonwealth; **Estados Unidos** United States
estadounidense *n., adj.* of or from the United States
estallar to explode
estampilla stamp; **coleccionar estampillas** to collect stamps
estanco tobacco shop
estante *m.* bookshelf
estantería *s.* shelves, bookcase
estar *irreg.* to be (P); **está despejado** it's clear (*weather*); **está lloviendo** it's raining; **está nevando** it's snowing; **está nublado** it's cloudy; **estar a buen precio** to be a good price; **estar a nombre de…** to be in … 's name; **estar al corriente** to be caught up (*with current events*); **estar celoso/a** to be jealous; **estar de acuerdo** to agree; **estar en (buena) forma** to be in (good) shape; **estar enfermo/a** to be sick; **estar listo/a** to be ready; **estar por** + *inf.* to be about to (*do something*); **estar seguro/a de** to be sure of; **estoy buscando…** I'm looking for …; **sólo estoy mirando** I'm just looking
estatua statue
estatura: de estatura mediana of medium height
estatus *m.* status
este *m.* east; **al este de** to the east of
este/a *adj.* this; *pron.* this (one); **esta noche** tonight
este… uh … (*pause sound*)
estelar: hora estelar prime time
estéreo (portátil) (portable) stereo

estereotipado/a stereotyped
estereotipo *n.* stereotype
estilo style
estimar to think highly of
estimulante stimulating
estimular to stimulate
estímulo stimulus
esto *neut. pron.* this
estómago stomach
estos/as *adj.* these; *pron.* these (ones)
estrategia strategy
estratégico/a strategic
estrecho/a close
estrella star
estrenar to debut
estreno debut
estrés *m.* stress; **sufrir de estrés** to suffer from stress
estresado/a stressed
estricto/a strict
estrofa verse
estructura structure
estructural structural
estudiante *m., f.* student (P)
estudiantil *adj.* student; **centro estudiantil** student center/union; **residencia estudiantil** dormitory (P)
estudiar to study; **estudio…** I study . . . , I'm studying . . . (P); **¿qué estudias?** what are you (*fam. s.*) studying?
estudio study; *pl.* studies, schooling; **estudios de posgrado** graduate studies; **estudios interdepartamentales** interdisciplinary studies (P); **estudios latinos** Latino studies (P); **estudios sobre el género** gender studies (P)
estudioso/a studious
estufa stove
estupendo/a stupendous
estupidez *f.* (*pl.* **estupideces**) stupid thing
etapa step, stage
ética *s.* ethics
etíope *adj. m., f.* Ethiopian
etiqueta etiquette
etnicidad *f.* ethnicity

étnico/a ethnic
etnografía ethnography, study of the races of people
Europa Europe
europeo/a *adj.* European
evaluación *f.* evaluation
evaluar (**evalúo**) to evaluate
evento event
evidencia evidence
evidente evident
evitar to avoid
evolucionar to evolve
exacto/a exact
exageración *f.* exaggeration
exagerado/a exaggerated
exagerar to exaggerate
examen *m.* test; **examen médico** medical exam
examinar to examine
excavación *f.* excavation
excelencia excellence
excelente excellent
excéntrico/a eccentric
excepción *f.* exception
excepcional exceptional
excepto *adv.* except
excesivo/a excessive
excluir (**y**) to exclude
exclusivo/a exclusive
excursión *f.* excursión; **ir** (*irreg.*) **de excursión** to go on a hike, go hiking
excusa excuse
exhibir to exhibit
exigencias *pl.* demands
exigente demanding
exigir (**j**) to demand
exilado/a exiled
exilio exile
existir to exist
éxito success; **tener** (*irreg.*) **éxito** to be successful
exitoso/a successful
exótico/a exotic; strange
expandir to expand
expansión *f.* expansion
expectativa expectation; **tener** (*irreg.*) **expectativas** to have expectations
expedir (**i, i**) to expedite; to issue
experiencia *n.* experience

experimentar to test, try out; to experience
experimento experiment
experto/a *n., adj.* expert
explicación *f.* explanation
explicar (**qu**) to explain
exploración *f.* exploration
explorador(a) explorer
explorar to explore
explosión *f.* explosion
explosivo/a explosive
explotar to exploit
exponer (*like* **poner**) to expose, report
exportación *f.* exportation; **productos de exportación** export products
exportador(a) exporter
exportar to export
expresar to express
expresión *f.* expression
expulsado/a expelled; thrown out
expulsar to eject
exquisito/a exquisite
extender (**ie**) to extend
extendido/a extended; **familia extendida** extended family
extensión *f.* extension
exterior *m.* exterior
extinción *f.* extinction; **especies** (*f. pl.*) **en peligro de extinción** endangered species
extranjero *n.* abroad; **ir** (*irreg.*) **al extranjero** to go abroad
extranjero/a *n.* foreigner, *adj.* foreign
extrañar to miss (*someone*); to be strange
extraño/a strange
extraordinario/a extraordinary
extraviar (**extravío**) to lose (*something*)
extremista *n., adj. m., f.* extremist
extremo *n.* extreme
extrovertido/a extroverted

F

fábrica factory
fabricado/a manufactured; **bienes** (*m. pl.*) **fabricados** manufactured goods
fabricar (**qu**) to make

fácil easy
facilidad *f.* ease; facility
facilitar to facilitate, make easy
factor *m.* factor, cause
facturar el equipaje to check luggage
facultad *f.* department (P)
falda skirt
falla error
falsificado/a falsified
falso/a false
falta *n.* lack
faltar to be missing, lacking
familia family; **familia extendida** extended family; **visitar a la familia** to visit one's family
familiar *adj. pertaining to a family*
famoso/a famous
fanático/a fan, enthusiast
fantástico/a fantastic
farmacéutico/a *n.* pharmacist; *adj.* pharmaceutical; **producto farmacéutico** pharmaceutical product
farmacia pharmacy
fascinante fascinating
fascinar to love, be fascinated by
fatal awful
fatiga fatigue
favor *m.* favor; **hacerle** (*irreg.*) **un favor a alguien** to do someone a favor; **por favor** please
favorecer (zc) to favor
favorito/a favorite
fax *m.*: **máquina fax** fax machine
febrero February
fecha date (*calendar*)
federal: distrito federal federal district
felicidad *f.* happiness
felicitación *f.* congratulations; **tarjeta de felicitación** greeting card
felicitar to congratulate
feliz (*pl.* **felices**) happy
femenino/a feminine
fenómeno phenomenon
feo/a ugly
fertilizante *m.* fertilizer
festivo: día (*m.*) **festivo** holiday
fiar (fío) to trust; **(no) ser** (*irreg.*) **de fiar** to be (un)reliable

ficción *f.* fiction; **ciencia ficción** science fiction
fiebre *f.* fever; **tener** (*irreg.*) **fiebre** to have a fever
fiel faithful
fiesta party; **dar** (*irreg.*) **una fiesta** to throw a party; **Fiesta de las Luces** Hanukkah; **fiesta de sorpresa** surprise party
fiestero/a fond of parties
figura figure
fijar to arrange, set up; **fijarse en** to take note of, notice
fijo/a fixed; **precio fijo** fixed price
filete *m.* fillet
filmación *f.* filming
filmar to film
filosofía philosophy (P)
filosófico/a philosophical
fin *m.* end; **con fines de lucro** for profit; **fin de semana** weekend; **poner** (*irreg.*) **fin a** to end; **por fin** finally
final *m.* end; *adj.* final
finalizar (c) to finalize
finanzas (*pl.*) **personales** personal finances
firmar to sign
física *s.* physics (P)
físico/a physicist; **estado físico** physical condition
flagrante flagrant
flan *m.* flan (*baked custard*)
flexible flexible
flor *f.* flower
florecer (zc) to flourish
florido/a flowery; **Pascua Florida** Easter
fluvial *adj. related to rivers*
fólico: ácido fólico folic acid
folleto brochure
fondo fund
forestal *adj.* forest
forjar to create
forma form, shape; **estar** (*irreg.*) **en (buena) forma** to be in (good) shape
formación *f.* formation
formar to form
formato format
foro forum
fortalecer (zc) to strengthen

fortuna luck
forzado/a forced
fósil *m.* fossil; **combustibles** (*m.*) **fósiles** fossil fuels
foto picture; **sacar (qu) fotos** to take pictures
foto(grafía) photo(graph); photography
fotografiado/a photographed
fotógrafo/a photographer
fracasar to fail
fracaso failure
frágil fragile
francamente frankly
francés *m.* French (*language*) (P)
francés, francesa *n., adj.* French
franja strip (*of land*)
frase *f.* phrase
frecuencia frecuency; **con frecuencia** frequently
frecuente frequent
fregar (ie) (gu) to clean
frente a *prep.* in the face of; versus; facing
fresco/a fresh cool; **hace fresco** it's cool (*weather*)
frijol *m.* bean
frío *n.*: **hace (mucho) frío** it's (very) cold (*weather*)
frío/a *adj.* cold
frito/a (*p.p. of* **freír**) fried; **huevo frito** fried egg; **papas fritas** French fries
frontera border
frustración *f.* frustration
frustrado/a frustrated
frustrar(se) to frustrate
fruta fruit; **barra de frutas** fruit bar
frutería fruit store
fuego fire; **arma** (*f.* [*but* **el arma**]) **de fuego** firearm
fuente *f.* source; fountain
fuera de outside (of); **por fuera** (on the) outside
fuerte strong
fuerza strength
fumar to smoke
función *f.* function
funcionar to function, work (*machines*)
fundación *f.* foundation; founding
fundamental basic

funicular *m.* funicular, railway
furioso/a furious
fusilamiento shooting
fútbol *m.* soccer; **fútbol americano** football
futbolista *m., f.* soccer player
futuro *n.* future
futuro/a *adj.* future

G

gallego Galician (*language spoken in the region of Galicia in northwest Spain*)
galleta cookie; **galleta salada** cracker
gallina hen; **ponérsele** (*irreg.*) **la piel de gallina a alguien** to get goosebumps
gamba shrimp (*Sp.*)
ganador(a) winner
ganancias *pl.* earnings
ganar to win; to earn
ganas *pl.:* **tener** (*irreg.*) **ganas de** + *inf.* to feel like (*doing something*)
ganga bargain
garaje *m.* garage
garantizar (c) to guarantee
garganta throat
gárgaras *pl.:* **hacer** (*irreg.*) **gárgaras** to gargle
gasolina gasoline
gastar to spend
gastos *pl.* expenses
gastronomía gastronomy, cuisine
gato/a cat
gemelo/a twin
gemir (i, i) to groan, moan; to howl
genealógico/a genealogical; **árbol** (*m.*) **genealógico** family tree
generación *f.* generation
general: **en general** in general
generalización *f.* generalization
generar to generate
genérico/a generic
género gender; genre; **estudios sobre el género** gender studies (P)
generoso/a generous
gente *f. s.* people; **rozarse (c) con la gente** to mingle with people; **tener** (*irreg.*) **don de gentes** to have a way with people

geografía geography
geográfico/a geographical
geometría geometry
gerente *m., f.* manager
gesto gesture
gimnasia: **hacer** (*irreg.*) **gimnasia** to work out
gimnasio gymnasium
globalizado/a globalized
gobernador(a) governor
gobierno government
golf *m.* golf
golfo gulf
gordito/a chubby
gordo/a fat
gorra baseball cap
gozar (c) de to enjoy
grabar to record
gracias thank you; **dar** (*irreg.*) **las gracias** to thank; **Día** (*m.*) **de Acción de Gracias** Thanksgiving
gracioso/a funny
graduación *f.* graduation
graduarse (me gradúo) to graduate
gramática grammar
gran, grande large, big, great; **creo que le queda un poco grande** I think it's a bit big on you; **Gran Bretaña** Great Britain
granola: **barra de granola** granola bar
grasa *n.* fat
grasoso/a greasy
gratis *adv. inv.* free (*of charge*)
grave serious
gregario/a gregarious
grifo tap, faucet; **agua** (*m.*) **del grifo** tap water
gris gray
gritar to yell, shout
grosero/a rude
grueso/a thick
grupo group
guapo/a handsome; good-looking
guaraní *m.* Guarani (*indigenous language of Paraguay*)
guardar (documentos) to keep, save (documents); **guardar(le) rencor (a alguien)** to hold a grudge (against someone)
guatemalteco/a *n., adj.* Guatemalan

guerra war; **guerra civil** civil war; **Guerra Fría** Cold War
guía *m., f.* guide (*person*); *f.* guidebook
guiar (guío) to guide
guisante *m.* pea
guitarra guitar; **tocar (qu) la guitarra** to play the guitar
gustar(le) to be pleasing (*to someone*); **me gusta...** I like . . .; **te gusta...** you (*fam. s.*) like . . .
gusto taste; pleasure; **mucho gusto** pleased to meet you (P)

H

haber *irreg.* to have (*aux.*)
habichuela bean
hábil skillful; proficient; **ser** (*irreg.*) **hábil para (las matemáticas, las ciencias)** to be good at (math, science)
habilidad *f.* ability; skill
habitación *f.* (dorm) room
habitante *m., f.* inhabitant
habitar to live
hablante *m., f.* speaker
hablar to speak; **hablar a espaldas de alguien** to talk behind someone's back
hacer *irreg.* (*p.p.* **hecho/a**) to make; to do; **hace** + *time* *time* ago; **hace** + *time* + **que** + *present* it's been (*time*) since . . .; **hace (mucho tiempo)** (a long time) ago; **hace... años** . . . years ago; **hace buen/mal tiempo** it's good/bad weather; **hace (mucho) calor/frío** it's (very) hot/cold; **hace fresco** it's cool (*weather*); **hace sol** it's sunny; **hace (mucho) viento** it's (very) windy; **hacer autostop** to hitchhike; **hacer camping** to go camping; **hacer ciclismo estacionario** to ride a stationary bike; **hacer clic** to click; **hacer cola** to stand in line; **hacer ejercicio** to exercise; **hacer ejercicio aeróbico** to do aerobics; **hacer el salto bungee** to bungee jump; **hacer escala** to make a stopover (*on a flight*);

hacer gárgaras to gargle; **hacer gimnasia** to work out; **hacer kayak** to kayak; **hacer la cama** to make the bed; **hacer la maleta** to pack a suitcase; **hacer las paces con** to make up with; **hacer novillos** to skip/cut school; **hacer rafting** to go rafting; **hacer trucos** to do tricks; **hacer un viaje** to take a trip; **hacer una búsqueda** to do a search; **hacer** *zapping* to channel surf; **hacerle un favor a alguien** to do someone a favor; **hacerse cargo de** to take charge (*of something*); **¿qué carrera haces?** what's your (*fam. s.*) major? (P)

hacia toward

hambre *f.* (*but* **el hambre**) hunger; **tener** (*irreg.*) **hambre** to be hungry

hamburguesa hamburger

hámster *m.* hamster

hasta *prep.* until; **de las… hasta las…** from (*hour*) to (*hour*); **hasta luego** until (see you) later; **hasta que** *conj.* until

hay (*from* **haber**): **(no) hay** there is/are (not) (P); **hay que** + *inf.* it's necessary + *inf.*

hechicero/a *adj.* magic; bewitching

hecho *n.* fact; **de hecho** in fact

hecho/a (*p.p. of* **hacer**) made; done

helado *n.* ice cream; **té** (*m.*) **helado** iced tea

hemisferio hemisphere

hepatitis *f.* hepatitis

heredar to inherit

herencia heritage; inheritance

herida *n.* wound

hermanastro/a stepbrother, stepsister

hermandad (*f.*) **de mujeres** sorority

hermano/a brother, sister; **medio/a hermano/a** half brother, half sister; *m. pl.* siblings

herramienta tool

hídrico/a of or related to water

hierba herb; grass

hígado liver

hijastro/a stepson, stepdaughter

hijo/a son, daughter; **hijo/a único/a** only child; *m. pl.* children

hipertensión *f.* hypertension

hipoteca mortgage; **amortizar (c) una hipoteca** to pay off a mortgage

hipotético/a hypothetical

hispano/a *n., adj.* Hispanic

Hispanoamérica Latin America

hispanohablante *m., f.* Spanish speaker

historia story; history (P)

histórico/a historical

historieta anecdote; short story; tale

hogar *m.* home

hoja leaf; sheet of paper; **hoja de papel aparte** separate piece of paper

¡hola! hello! hi! (P)

hombre *m.* man (P); **hombre de negocios** businessman

hombro shoulder

homenaje *m.* homage

homicidio homicide

homogéneo/a homogeneous

honesto/a honest, sincere

honor *m.* honor

hora hour; time; **a la misma hora** at the same time; **¿a qué hora… ?** at what time . . . ?; when . . . ?; **con dos horas de anticipación** two hours ahead of time; **¿qué hora es?** what time is it?; **¿tiene Ud. la hora?** do you (*form. s.*) have the time?; **¿tienes la hora?** do you (*fam. s.*) have the time?

horario schedule

hormiga ant

horno stove; **al horno** baked

horrible terrible, horrible

hospital *m.* hospital

hostilidad *f.* hostility

hotel *m.* hotel

hoy en día nowadays; **¿qué día es hoy?** what day is today?

hueso bone

huésped(a) guest

huevo egg; **huevo frito** fried egg; **huevos revueltos** scrambled eggs

humanidades *f., pl.* humanities (P)

humano human

humano/a *adj.* human; **derechos humanos** human rights

humilde humble

humillación *f.* humiliation

humo smoke

humor *m.* humor; mood; **estar** (*irreg.*) **de buen/mal humor** to be in a good/bad mood

huracán *m.* hurricane

I

Ibérico/a: Península Ibérica Iberian Peninsula

ida: de ida one-way; **de ida y vuelta** round-trip

idea idea; **es buena idea** it's a good idea

identificar (qu) to identify; **identificarse con** to identify with

idioma *m.* language (P)

iglesia church

igual equal; **al igual que** just like

igualmente likewise, same here (P)

ilegal illegal

imagen *f.* (*pl.* **imágenes**) image

imaginar to imagine

imaginario/a imaginary

imaginativo/a imaginative

impaciente impatient

impactar to have an impact

impacto *n.* impact

imperfecto *gram.* imperfect (tense)

imperio empire

impermeable *m.* raincoat

importado/a *n.* imported

importancia importance

importante important

importar to matter; to be important; **importarle un pito** not to care about

imposible impossible; **es imposible** it's impossible

impresión *f.* impression

imprimir to print

impuesto *n.* tax

impulsivo/a impulsive

impulso impulse

inadecuado/a inadequate

inanimado/a inanimate

inapropiado/a inappropriate

inca *n. m., f.* Inca

incaico/a Incan
incendio fire; **seguro contra incendios** fire insurance
incertidumbre f. uncertainty
incluir (y) to include
incluso/a including
incompleto/a incomplete
incontrolable uncontrollable
inconveniente inconvenient
incorporar to incorporate
increíble incredible, unbelievable
indefinido/a indefinite
independencia independence
independiente independent
independizarse (c) to become independent
indicador m. indicator
indicar (qu) to indicate
indiferencia indifference
indiferente indifferent
indígena n. m., f. indigenous (person); adj. m., f. indigenous, native
indigenismo indigenism
indio/a n. Indian
indirecto/a indirect
indiscreto indiscreet
indispensable essential
indómito/a untamed
indudablemente undoubtedly
industria industry
inesperado/a unexpected
inestabilidad f. instability
inestable unstable
infarto (cardíaco) heart attack
infiel adj. m., f. unfaithful
infierno hell
infinitivo/a gram. infinitive
inflación f. inflation
inflexión f. inflection
influencia influence
influir (y) en to influence
información f. information
informado/a informed
informarse to inform oneself
informática computer science (P)
informativo/a informative
informe m. report
infraestructura infrastructure
infringir (j) to infringe
infundado/a unfounded

ingeniería (civil/eléctrica/mecánica) (civil/electrical/mechanical) engineering (P)
ingeniero/a (civil, eléctrico/a, mecánico/a) (civil, electrical, mechanical) engineer
ingenuo/a naive
Inglaterra England
inglés n. m. English (language) (P)
inglés, inglesa adj. English
ingresos pl. income
inicial adj. initial
iniciar to initiate, begin
inmediatamente immediately
inmigración f. (ilegal) (illegal) immigration
inmigrante m., f. immigrant
inmobiliaria: agente (m., f.) de inmobiliaria real estate agent
inmóvil unmoving
inmunodeficiencia: SIDA (síndrome (m.) de inmunodeficiencia adquirida) AIDS (Acquired Immune Deficiency Syndrome)
inodoro toilet
inolvidable unforgettable
inquieto/a restless
inquilino/a tenant
insecto insect
inseguridad f. insecurity
inseguro/a insecure
insistir en to insist on
insolación f. heat stroke
inspirar to inspire
instalaciones f. pl. facilities
instalar to install; instalarse en to settle into (a house)
instantáneo/a: mensajero instantáneo instant messenger
instituto institute
instrucción f. instruction
insuficiente insufficient
integración f. integration
integridad f. integrity
inteligencia intelligence
inteligente intelligent
intención f. intention
intenso/a intense
intentar to try
interacción f. interaction

intercambiar to exchange
intercambio n. exchange
interdepartamental: estudios interdepartamentales interdisciplinary studies (P)
interés m. interest; pl. interest (finance); tipos de interés interest rates
interesante interesting
interesar to interest, be interesting
interior adj. interior
internacional international; noticias (pl.) internacionales international news
internar to confine
Internet m. Internet
interno/a internal; órgano interno internal organ
interpretación f. interpretation
interpretar to interpret, explain
interrogativo/a interrogative
intimidad f. intimacy
íntimo/a intimate, private; close (relationship)
intoxicante poisonous; intoxicating
introducir (zc) to introduce
introvertido/a introverted
inundación f. flood
invadir to invade
invasión f. invasion
inventar to invent
invernadero greenhouse; efecto Invernadero greenhouse effect
inversión f. investment
invertir (ie, i) to invest
investigación f. research
investigador(a) researcher
investigar (gu) to research
invierno winter
invitado/a guest
invitar to invite
inyección f. injection; ponerle (irreg.) una inyección (a alguien) to give (someone) a shot
ir irreg. to go; ir a to go to; ir a un concierto to go to a concert; ir a un parque de diversiones to go to an amusement park; ir al cine to go to the movies; ir al extranjero to go abroad; ir de excursión to go on a hike, go hiking

irresponsable irresponsible
irritado/a irritated
irritante irritating, annoying
irritar(se) to irritate (get irritated)
isla island
italiano/a *n., adj.* Italian
izquierda *n.* left-hand side; **a la izquierda de** to the left of; **doblar a la izquierda** to turn left

J

jabón *m.* soap
jamás never, not ever
jamón *m.* ham
japonés, japonesa *n., adj.* Japanese
jarabe *m.* **(para la tos)** (cough) syrup
jardín *m.* garden
jefe/a boss, chief
jerga slang, jargon
jitomate *m.* tomato (*Mex.*)
jornada work day; **de media jornada** part-time
joven *n. m., f.* (*pl.* **jóvenes**) young person; *adj.* young
joya jewel
joyería jewelry store
jubilado/a retired
jubilarse to retire
judías verdes green beans
judío/a: pascua de los judíos Passover (4A)
juego game; **juego de charadas** charades
jueves *m. inv.* Thursday
juez(a) (*m. pl.* **jueces**) judge
jugador(a) player
jugar (ue) (gu) to play; **jugar a los videojuegos** to play video games; **jugar al escondite** to play hide and seek
jugo juice
julio July
junio June
junto/a together
jurado panel of judges
jurar to swear (*an oath*)
justificar (qu) to justify
justo/a *adj.* fair
juvenil *adj.* youth

juventud *f.* youth
juzgar (gu) to judge

K

kayak: hacer (*irreg.*) **kayak** to kayak
kilo(grama) *m.* kilogram
kilómetro kilometer

L

la *f. def. art.* the (P); *d.o.* her, it, you (*f. form. s.*); **a la una** at one o'clock; **es la una** it's one o'clock
labio lip
laboratorio laboratory
lacio/a: pelo lacio straight hair
lácteo/a dairy; **producto lácteo** dairy product
lado *n.* side; **al lado de** beside
ladrillo brick
lago lake
lamer to lick
lámpara lamp
lana wool
langosta lobster
lanza: punta de lanza spearhead
lanzar (c) to throw, fling; **lanzarse a** break into (*career*)
lápiz *m.* (*pl.* **lápices**) pencil (P)
largo/a long; **a lo largo de** throughout; **de largo plazo** long-term
las *f. pl.* the (P); *d.o.* you (*f. form. pl.*); them; **a las…** at . . . o'clock
lástima compassion; shame; **lástima que…** too bad that . . .
lastimar(se) to hurt (oneself)
lata de aluminio aluminum can
latino/a *adj.* Latino, Latina; **estudios latinos** Latino studies (P)
Latinoamérica Latin America
latinoamericano/a *n., adj.* Latin American
lavabo sink (bathroom)
lavadora washing machine
lavaplatos *m. inv.* dishwasher
lavar to wash; **lavarse los dientes** to brush one's teeth
le *i.o. s.* to/for him, her, it, you (*form. s.*)
leal loyal
lealtad *f.* loyalty

lección *f.* lesson
leche *f.* milk; **café** (*m.*) **con leche** coffee with milk
lechuga lettuce
lector(a) reader
lectura *n.* reading
leer (y) to read
legalmente legally
legítimo/a legitimate
lejano/a distant, far
lejía *n.* bleach
lejos de *adv.* far away from
lengua tongue; language (P); **lengua extranjera** foreign language; **sacar (qu) la lengua** to stick out one's tongue; **trabársele la lengua a alguien** to get tongue-tied
lenguaje *m.* language
lentes *m. pl.* glasses (*vision*)
lento/a slow
les *i.o. pl.* to/for you (*form. pl.*), them
letra letter (*of the alphabet*); lyrics; **letra cursiva** italics; *pl.* humanities
levantar to lift, raise up; **levantar pesas** to lift weights; **levantarse** to get up
léxico vocabulary
ley *f.* law
leyenda legend
liberal liberal
libertad *f.* liberty, freedom
libertino/a libertine
libra pound (*weight*)
libre free (unfettered); **al aire libre** outdoors; **Estado Libre Associado** Free Associated State, Commonwealth; **ratos libres** free time
librería bookstore (P)
libro book (P)
licencia license; **sacar (qu) la licencia de conducir** to get a driver's license
licor *m.* liquor
ligarse con to get together with
ligero/a *adj.* light
limitar to limit
límite *m.* limit
limón *m.* lemon
limonada lemonade

limpiar to clean; **limpiar la casa (entera)** to clean the (whole) house

limpieza *n.* cleaning; cleanliness; **producto de limpieza** cleaning product

lindo/a pretty

línea line; **línea aérea** airline; **patinar en línea** to inline skate

lingüístico/a linguistic

lío problem; **meterse en líos** to get into trouble

lista list

listo/a ready; clever, smart; **estar** (*irreg.*) **listo/a** to be ready; **ser** (*irreg.*) **listo/a** to be clever

literatura literature (P)

llamada *n.* (telephone) call

llamar to call; **¿cómo se llama (él/ella)?** what's his/her name? (P); **¿como te llamas?** what's your (*fam. s.*) name? (P); **llamar por teléfono** to call on the telephone; **llamarse** to be called; **me llamo…** my name is . . . (P)

llanura flatland, prairie

llave *n. f.* key

llegada arrival

llegar (gu) to arrive; **¿cómo se llega a… ?** how do you get to . . . ?; **llegar a tiempo** to arrive on time

llenar to fill

lleno/a full

llevar to take, carry; to wear (*clothing*); **llevar al / a la veterinario/a** to take to the veterinarian; **llevar… créditos** to have . . . credits; **llevarse bien/mal con** to get along well/poorly with

llorar to cry

llover (ue) to rain; **está lloviendo** it's raining; **llueve** it's raining

lluvia rain

lluvioso/a rainy; **bosque** (*m.*) **lluvioso** rain forest

lo *d.o.* him, it, you (*m. form. s.*); **lo que** what, that which

local local; **noticias locales** local news

localizador *m.* pager

localizarse (c) to be located

loco/a mad, crazy

lógico/a logical

lograr + *inf.* to succeed (*in doing something*)

lomo loin

longitud *f.* duration

loro parrot

los *def. art. m. pl.* the (P); *d.o.* them, you (*form. pl.*); **los años veinte (treinta)** the twenties (thirties); **los/lás demás** others

lucha *n.* fight; struggle

lucro: con fines de lucro for profit

luego then; **hasta luego** until (see you) later

lugar *m.* place

lujo luxury; **hotel** (*m.*) **de lujo** luxury hotel

lunar *m.*; **de lunares** polka-dotted

lunes *m. inv.* Monday; **el (los) lunes** on Monday(s)

luz *f.* (*pl.* **luces**) light (P); electricity; **Fiesta de las Luces** Hanukkah

M

madera wood

madrastra stepmother

madre *f.* mother; **madre soltera** single mother

madrina godmother

madrugada early morning hours

maestría *n.* mastery, skill; master's degree

maestro/a (de primaria, secundaria) (elementary, high school) teacher

magia *n.* magic

magos *pl.*: **los Reyes** (*m.*) **Magos** the Magi (Three Wise Men); **Día** (*m.*) **de los Reyes Magos** Epiphany (January 6), Day of the Magi

maíz *m.* corn; **palomitas de maíz** popcorn; **tortilla de maíz** corn tortilla

mal, malo/a *adj.* bad; sick; **caerle** (*irreg.*) **mal a alguien** to dislike someone; **hace mal tiempo** it's bad weather; **llevarse mal con** to get along poorly with; **manejar mal** to manage poorly; **pasarlo mal** to

have a bad time; **portarse mal** to misbehave; **quedarle mal** to fit poorly

maldad *n. f.* evil

maleta suitcase; **hacer** (*irreg.*) **la maleta** to pack a suitcase

maletero skycap, porter

maletín *m.* briefcase

malicioso/a malicious

mamá mom; mother

mandar to send; to order

mandato *n.* command

mando a distancia remote control

mandón, mandona bossy

manejar (bien/mal) to manage (well/poorly)

manera manner, way; **pensar (ie) de manera directa** to think in a direct (linear) manner

manifestación *f.* demonstration

manifestar(se) (ie) to manifest, show

manipular to manipulate

mano *f.* hand; **darse** (*irreg.*) **la mano** to shake hands

mansión *f.* mansion

mantel *m.* tablecloth

mantener (*like* **tener**) to maintain; to support; **mantenerse a raya** to keep (*something*) away

mantequilla butter; **mantequilla de cacahuete** peanut butter

manual *m.* workbook

manufacturado/a manufactured

manzana apple; city block

mañana *n.* morning; *adv.* tomorrow; **de la mañana** in the morning (A.M.); **hasta mañana** until (see you) tomorrow; **pasado mañana** the day after tomorrow; **por la mañana** in the morning

mapa *m.* map

máquina machine; **máquina fax** fax machine

mar *m., f.* sea, ocean

maravilloso/a marvelous

marca brand name

marcar (qu) to mark

mareado/a nauseated, dizzy

marearse to get nauseated, sick (*boat, car, plane*)

marido husband

marino/a *adj.* marine
mariscos *pl.* shellfish; seafood
marrón *adj. m., f.* brown
martes *m. inv.* Tuesday; **Martes de Carnaval** Mardi Gras
marzo March
más *adv.* more; **cada vez más** more and more; **es más** what's more; **más... que** more . . . than
mascota *n.* pet
masculino/a masculine
matar to kill
matemáticas mathematics (P)
materia subject (*school*) (P)
material *m.* material
materialista *m., f.* materialist
materno/a maternal
matrícula tuition
matrimonial: **cama matrimonial** queen bed
matrimonio matrimony, marriage
mayo May
mayor older; **el/la mayor** the oldest
mayoría majority
me *d.o.* me; *i.o.* to/for me; *refl. pron.* myself; **me gusta...** I like . . .; **me llamo** my name is (P); **me parece(n)...** it/that seems . . . to me; **¿me podría traer... ?** could you (*form. s.*) bring me . . . ?
mecánico/a mechanic; **ingeniería mecánica** mechanical engineering (P); **ingeniero/a mecánico/a** mechanical engineer
media *n.* average
mediano/a *adj.* medium; average; **de estatura mediana** of medium height
medianoche *f.* midnight; **a medianoche** at midnight
medias *pl.* stockings; pantyhose
medicación *f.* medication
medicina medicine
médico/a *n.* doctor; *adj.* medical; **examen** (*m.*) **médico** medical exam; **seguro médico** medical insurance; **servicios médicos** medical services
medidas *pl.* measures
medio *n. s.* means, middle; **medio ambiente** environment; **medios de comunicación** media

medio/a *adj.* half; middle; **clase** (*f.*) **media** middle class; **medio/a hermano/a** half brother/sister; **media pensión** room and one other meal (usually breakfast); **y media** half past (*hour*)
medioambiental environmental
mediodía *m.* noon, midday; **a mediodía** at noon
meditar to meditate
mediterráneo/a *adj.* Mediterranean
mejillas cheeks
mejor better
mejorar to improve
melodrama *m.* melodrama
membresía membership
memoria memory
memorizar (c) to memorize
mencionar to mention
mendigo/a beggar
menor younger; **el/la menor** the youngest
menos less; least; **a menos que** *conj.* unless; **menos cuarto** a quarter to (*hour*); **menos... que** less . . . than; **por lo menos** at least
mensaje *m.* message
mensajero/a messenger; **mensajero instantáneo** instant messenger
mensual monthly; **presupuesto mensual** monthly budget
mentalidad *f.* mentality
mente *f.* mind
mentir (ie, i) to lie
mentira lie
mentiroso/a liar
mentón *m.* chin
menú *m.* menu
menudo: **a menudo** often
mercadeo marketing
mercado market
mercancías *pl.* goods
merecer (zc) to deserve
merendar (ie) to snack
meridional southern
merienda *n.* snack
mérito merit; **atribuirse (y) todo el mérito** to take all the credit
mermelada jam

mes *m.* month; **cada mes** each month; **¿en qué mes cae... ?** ¿what month is . . . ?; **una vez al mes** once a month
mesa table (P)
mesero/a waiter, waitress
meseta plateau
mesita end table
mestizaje *m.* mixing of races
mestizo/a *n.* mixed-race person
meta goal; **alcanzar (c) una meta** to reach a goal
metales (*m.*) **preciosos** precious metals
meteorológico/a meteorological
meterse to pick a fight; **meterse en líos** to get into trouble
metódico/a methodical
metro meter; **metros cuadrados** square meters
mexicano/a *n., adj.* Mexican
mexicanoamericano/a *n., adj.* Mexican-American
mezcla mixture
mezquita mosque
mí *obj. of prep.*
mi(s) *poss.* my; **mi apellido es...** my last name is . . . (P); **mi nombre es...** my name is . . . (P)
microondas *m. s.* microwave
microscopio microscope
miedo fear; **tener(le)** (*irreg.*) **miedo (a alguien)** to be afraid (of someone)
miembro/a member
mientras *adv.* meanwhile; **mientras que** *conj.* while
miércoles *m. inv.* Wednesday
migración *f.* migration
migratorio/a migratory
mil thousand, one thousand
militar *adj.* military
milla mile
millón *m.* (de) million
millonario millionaire
mina *n.* mine
miniserie *f.* miniseries
minoría minority
minoritario/a *adj.* minority
minuto minute
mío/a/os/as *poss.* my, (of) mine

mirar to look (at), watch; **sólo estoy mirando** I'm just looking
misceláneo/a miscellaneous
misión f. mission
mismo/a same; self; **a la misma hora** at the same time
misterio mystery
mitad f. half
mito myth
mitología mythology
mixto/a mixed; **ensalada mixta** tossed salad
mochila backpack (P)
moda fashion; **de moda** in style
modelo model; m., f. model (fashion)
módem m. modem
modernización f. modernization
moderno/a modern
modesto/a modest
mojado/a wet
molestar to bother
momento moment, instant
moneda currency, coin, **coleccionar monedas** to collect coins
monitor m. monitor
monótono/a monotonous
montaña mountain; **escalar montañas** to go mountain climbing
montar a caballo to go horseback riding
morado/a purple
mórbido/a morbid
morder (ue) to bite
moreno/a dark-skinned
morir(se) (ue, u) (p.p. **muerto/a**) to die; **ya murió** he/she already died
moro/a n. Moor; adj. Moorish
morrón m. blow, bang, hit
mortalidad f. mortality
mosquetero: los Tres Mosqueteros The Three Musketeers
mostrador m. counter (kitchen, etc.)
mostrar (ue) to show (something to someone)
motivo motive, reason
motor m. engine, motor
mover (ue) to move (around); **moverse** to move (houses)
móvil: teléfono móvil cell phone

movimiento movement
mozo bellhop
muchacho/a boy, girl
mucho adv. a lot, much
mucho/a adj. much, a lot (of); **hace mucho calor** it's very hot; **hace mucho frío** it's very cold; **hace mucho viento** it's very windy; **mucho gusto** pleased to meet you (P); **pasar mucho tiempo** to spend a lot of time
mudanza move
mudarse to move (to another house)
mueble m. piece of furniture
muerte f. death; **pena de muerte** death penalty
muerto/a (p.p. of **morir**) dead
muestra example
mujer f. woman (P); wife; **hermandad** (f.) **de mujeres**, sorority, **mujer de negocios** businesswoman; **mujer policía** policewoman; **mujer político** (female) politician; **mujer química** (female) chemist; **mujer soldado** (female) soldier
mujeriego n. womanizer
muleta crutch
multa fee, fine
multinacional multinational
mundial adj. world
mundo world, **mundo de los espectáculos** entertainment industry
muñeca wrist; doll
muro wall
músculo muscle
museo museum; **visitar un museo** to visit a museum
música music (P)
músico/a musician
musulmán, musulmana n., adj. Muslim
muy very

N

nacer (zc) to be born
nacido/a born; **recién nacido/a** newborn baby
nacimiento birth
nación f. nation

nacional national; **noticias** (pl.) **nacionales** national news; **producto nacional bruto** gross national product
nada nothing; none
nadador(a) swimmer
nadar to swim
nadie nobody, not anybody
nahuatl m. Nahuatl (language of the Aztecs)
naranja orange (fruit)
nariz f. nose; **tener** (irreg.) **la nariz tapada** to have a stuffed-up nose
narración f. narration
narrar to narrate
natación f. swimming
nativo/a adj. native, indigenous
natural adj. natural; **ciencias naturales** natural sciences (P); **desastre** (m.) **natural** natural disaster; **recursos naturales** natural resources
naturaleza nature
navegar (gu) (la red) to navigate; to surf (the Web); **navegar en barco** to sail
Navidad f. Christmas
navideño/a adj. Christmas
necesario/a necessary; **es necesario** it's necessary
necesidad f. necessity
necesitar to need; **necesitar** + inf. to need to (do something)
neerlandés, neerlandesa adj. Dutch
negación f. negation
negar (ie) (gu) to deny
negativo/a adj. negative
negocio business; **hombre** (m.) **de negocios** businessman; **mujer** (f.) **de negocios** businesswoman
negrita: en negrita in boldface type
negro/a adj. black
nervioso/a nervous
nevar (ie) to snow; **está nevando** it's snowing; **nieva** it's snowing
nevera freezer
ni... ni neither . . . nor
nieto/a grandson, granddaughter; pl. grandchildren
ningún, ninguno/a adj. no, not any
ninguno/a pron. none, not any

niñero/a baby-sitter; nanny

niñez *f.* (*pl.* **niñeces**) childhood

niño/a child; boy, girl

nivel *m.* level; **nivel económico** economic level

no no; not; **no aguantar** not to be able to stand, put up with; **no es cierto** it's not true; **no es posible** it's not possible; **no es seguro/a** it's not sure; **no es verdad** it's not true; **no obstante** nevertheless; **no ser de fiar** to be unreliable; **todavía no sé** I still don't know (P); **ya no** no longer

noche *f.* night; **buenas noches** good night (P); **de la noche** in the evening (night); **esta noche** tonight; **Noche Vieja** New Year's Eve; **por la noche** in the evening (night); **todas las noches** every night

Nochebuena Christmas Eve

nocivo/a unhealthy, noxious

nocturno/a *adj.* nighttime

nombrar to name

nombre *m.* name; **estar** (*irreg.*) **a nombre de...** to be in . . . 's name; **mi nombre es...** my name is . . . (P)

nominar to nominate

norma norm

norte *m.* north; **al norte de** to the north of

Norteamérica North America

norteamericano/a *n., adj.* North American (*from the United States or Canada*)

nos *d.o.* us; *i.o.* to/for us; *refl. pron.* ourselves; **nos vemos** see you around

nosotros/as *sub. pron.* we (P); *obj. of prep.* us

nostálgico/a nostalgic

nota note

notable good

notar to note, notice

noticia piece of news; *pl.* news; **noticias (internacionales, locales, nacionales)** (international, local, national) news

noticiero newscast, news show

novecientos/as nine hundred

novecientos mil nine hundred thousand

novedoso/a *adj.* novel

novela *n.* novel

novelista *m., f.* novelist

noventa ninety

noviazgo engagement

noviembre November

novillos: hacer (*irreg.*) **novillos** to skip/cut school

novio/a boyfriend, girlfriend; bride, groom

nube *f.* cloud

nublado/a cloudy; **está nublado** it's cloudy

nublar to darken

nudista *adj. m., f.* nudist

nuestro/a/os/as *poss.* our

nueve nine

nuevo/a new

nuez (*pl.* **nueces**) nut

número number; **¿qué número calza?** what size shoe do you (*form. s.*) wear?

numeroso/a numerous

nunca never, not ever; **casi nunca** almost never

O

o or; **o... o** either . . . or

ó or (*used between two numbers to avoid confusion with zero*)

obedecer (zc) to obey

obediencia obedience

obediente obedient

objetividad *f.* objectivity

objetivo/a objective

objeto *n.* object

obligación *f.* obligation

obligar (gu) to obligate, require

obligatorio/a required

obra *n.* work (of art)

observación *f.* observation

observador(a) observer

obsesión *f.* obsession

obstáculo obstacle

obstante: no obstante nevertheless

obtener (*like* **tener**) to obtain, get

obvio/a obvious

ocasión *f.* occasion

ocasionar to cause

occidental *adj.* western

océano ocean; **océano Pacífico** Pacific Ocean

ochenta eighty

ocho eight

ochocientos/as eight hundred

ochocientos mil eight hundred thousand

ocio leisure time

octubre October

ocultar(le) secretos (a alguien) to hide secrets (from someone)

ocupación *f.* occupation

ocupado/a busy

ocupar to occupy

ocurrir to occur

odiar to hate

odio hatred

oeste *m.* west; **al oeste de** to the west of

ofender(se) to offend (get offended)

ofensivo/a offensive

oferta *n.* offer

oficina office (P)

oficio job, profession; trade

ofrecer (zc) to offer

oír *irreg.* to hear

ojalá que I hope, wish that

ojo eye

oleada *n.* wave

oliva: aceite (*m.*) **de oliva** olive oil

olvidar to forget

once eleven

opción *f.* option

operación *f.* operation

opinar to think, believe

opinión *f.* opinion

oportunidad *f.* opportunity

optativo/a optional

optimista *n. m., f.* optimist; *adj.* optimistic

opuesto/a opposite

oración *f.* sentence

orden *m.* order (*chronological*); **poner** (*irreg.*) **las cosas en orden** to put things in order

ordenador *m.* computer (*Sp.*)

ordenar to order, put in order

orejas (outer) ears

orgánico/a organic

organismo organism

organización *f.* organization
organizado/a organized
organizar (c) to organize
órgano organ; **órgano interno** internal organ
orgullo pride
orgulloso/a (de) proud (of)
orientación *f.* orientation, direction
origen *m.* (*pl.* **orígenes**) origin; **¿de qué origen es/son... ?** what is/are . . . 's (national) origin?
os *d.o.* you (*fam. pl. Sp.*); *i.o.* to/for you (*fam. pl. Sp.*); *refl. pron.* yourselves (*fam. pl. Sp.*)
oscurecer (zc) to get dark
oscuro/a dark
oso *n.* bear
otoño fall (*season*)
otorgar (gu) to award
otro/a other; another
oyente *m., f.* listener
ozono ozone; **capa de ozono** ozone layer

P

paciencia patience
paciente *m., f.* patient; *adj.* patient
pacífico/a peaceful; **océano Pacífico** Pacific Ocean
padecer (zc) de to suffer from
padrastro stepfather
padre *m.* father; *pl.* parents; **padre soltero** single father
padrino godfather; **padrino de boda** groomsman
pagar (gu) to pay (for); **pagar a plazos** to pay in installments; **pagar de una vez** to pay off all at once
página page; **página web** Web page
pago payment
país *m.* country; **país desarrollado** developed country; **país en vías de desarrollo** developing country; **País Vasco** Basque country; **los Países Bajos** The Netherlands
paisaje *m.* landscape
paisajista *adj. m., f.:* **arquitectura paisajista** landscape architecture
pájaro bird
palabra word

palabrota swear word
palomitas (*pl.*) **de maíz** popcorn
pampa pampa, prairie
pan *m.* bread; **pan dulce** sweet bread (*Mex.*); **pan tostado** toast
pana corduroy
panadería bakery
panceta *Arg.* bacon
panqueque *m.* pancake
pantalla screen (*movie, computer*) (P)
pantalón, pantalones *m.* pants; **pantalones cortos** shorts
papa potato; **papas fritas** French fries; **puré** (*m.*) **de papas** mashed potatoes
papá *m.* dad, father; daddy
papel *m.* role, part; paper; **hoja de papel aparte** separate piece of paper; **toalla de papel** paper towel
papitas *pl.* potato chips
paquete *m.* package
par *m.* pair; **un par de** a couple of
para for; in order to; **para + inf.** in order to (*do something*); **para que** so that
paracaidismo skydiving; **practicar (qu) el paracaidismo** to skydive
parada de autobuses bus stop
paráfrasis *f.* paraphrase
paraguayo/a *n., adj.* Paraguayan
parapente *m.:* **practicar (qu) el parapente** to hang glide
parar to stop
parcial biased; **ser** (*irreg.*) **parcial** to be biased
parcialidad *f.* bias
parecer (zc) to look; to seem (like); **me parece(n)...** it/that seems . . . to me; **parece ser** it seems to be, he/she seems . . .; **parecerse (a)** to resemble
parecido/a (a) similar (to)
pared *f.* wall; **pintar las paredes** to paint the walls
pareja couple; mate; partner; *pl.* pairs
paréntesis *m. inv.* parenthesis
pariente *m., f.* relative
parque *m.* park; **ir** (*irreg.*) **a un parque de diversiones** to go to an amusement park

párrafo paragraph
parte *f.* part; **partes del cuerpo** parts of the body
participar to participate
particular particular; private; **casa particular** private residence
partido game; **partido político** political party
pasa raisin
pasado/a *adj.* past; spoiled (*food*); **pasado mañana** the day after tomorrow
pasajero/a *n.* passenger
pasaporte *m.* passport
pasar (mucho) tiempo to pass, spend (a lot of) time; **pasar a ser** to become; **pasar la aspiradora** to vacuum; **pasar por la aduana** to go through customs; **pasar por seguridad** to go through security; **pasarlo bien/mal** to have a good/bad time
pasatiempo pastime
Pascua: Pascua (de los judíos) Passover; **Pascua (Florida)** Easter
pasear to walk, stroll; **sacar (qu) a pasear** to take for a walk
paseo *n.* walk, stroll; **dar** (*irreg.*) **un paseo** to take a walk
pasión *f.* passion
paso step
pastel *m.* pastry; cake; *pl.* pastries; **porción** (*f.*) **de pastel** slice of cake
pastilla pill
patata potato (*Sp.*)
paterno/a paternal
patinar (en línea) to (inline) skate
patio courtyard, patio
patria homeland
Patricio: Día (*m.*) **de San Patricio** St. Patrick's Day
patrio/a patriotic
pavo turkey
paz *f.* (*pl.* **paces**) peace; **dejar en paz** to leave alone; **hacer** (*irreg.*) **las paces** to make up with
peca *n.* freckle
pecado *n.* sin
pecho chest; **tomarse algo muy a pecho** to take something to heart; to feel something intensely

peculiaridad *f.* peculiarity
pedagogía pedagogy; education
pedazo piece
pedir (i, i) to ask for, request; to order (*restaurant*); **pedir ayuda** to ask for help; **pedir disculpas** to apologize (*to someone*); **pedir prestado/a** to borrow
pegado/a stuck on; close together
peinado hairdo
peinar to comb
pelar to peel
pelearse to fight
película movie; **ver** (*irreg.*) **una película** to watch a movie
peligro danger; **especies** (*f. pl.*) **en peligro de extinción** endangered species
peligroso/a dangerous
pelirrojo/a red-headed
pelo (canoso/lacio/rizado/rubio) (gray/straight/curly/blond) hair
pelotero/a: ser (*irreg.*) **pelotero/a** to be a kiss-up
pena shame; penalty; sorrow; **pena de muerte** death penalty
península Ibérica Iberian Peninsula
pensar (ie) to think; **pensar de** to think of; **pensar de manera directa** to think in a direct (linear) manner; **pensar en** to think about
pensión *f.* boardinghouse; **media pensión** room and one other meal (usually breakfast); **pensión completa** room and all meals
peor worse
pepino (de mar) (sea) cucumber
pequeñeces *f. pl.* little things
pequeño/a little, small
per cápita: renta per cápita per capita income
perder (ie) to lose; **perder peso** to lose weight
pérdida loss; **pérdida de tiempo** waste of time; **pérdida de valores tradicionales** loss of traditional values
perdón *m.* forgiveness
perdonable forgivable
perdonar to forgive; to pardon, excuse

perezoso/a lazy
perfeccionista *m., f.* perfectionist
perfecto/a perfect
perfil *m.* profile
periférico peripheral device
periódico newspaper
periodista *m., f.* journalist
permiso permission
permitir to allow
pero but
perpetuar (perpetúo) to perpetuate
perplejo/a perplexed; **dejar perplejo/a (a alguien)** to leave (someone) perplexed
perro dog
persistente persistent
persona person
personaje *m.* character (*fictional*)
personal personal; **finanzas personales** personal finances; **respetar el espacio personal** to respect personal space
personalidad *f.* personality
perspectiva perspective
pertenecer (zc) to belong
peruano/a Peruvian
pesa weight; **levantar pesas** to lift weights
pesado/a heavy
pesar(se) to weigh (oneself); **a pesar de** *prep.* in spite of, despite
pescado fish (*food*)
pescar (qu) to fish
pesimista *n. m., f.* pessimist; *adj.* pessimistic
peso weight; **bajar de peso** to lose weight; **perder (ie) peso** to lose weight
pesquero/a *adj.* fishing
pesticida pesticide
petróleo petroleum (oil)
pez *m.* (*pl.* **peces**) fish (*alive*)
piano piano; **tocar (qu) el piano** to play the piano
picante hot, spicy
picar (qu) to bite; to nibble
picoso/a spicy
pie *m.* foot; **a pie** on foot; **dedo del pie** toe; **pies cuadrados** square feet

piel *f.* skin; **ponérsele** (*irreg.*) **la piel de gallina a alguien** to get goosebumps
pierna leg
pijama *m. s.* pajamas
pila (recargable) (rechargeable) battery
piloto/a pilot
pinchado/a: rueda pinchada flat tire
pintar to paint; **pintar las paredes** to paint the walls
pintor(a) painter
pintoresco/a picturesque
pirámide *f.* pyramid
piscina swimming pool
piso floor; flat, apartment (*Sp.*); **barrer el piso** to sweep the floor
pista track
pito: importarle un pito not to care about
pizarra chalkboard (P)
pizza pizza; **porción** (*f.*) **de pizza** slice of pizza
placer *m.* pleasure
plancha iron
planchar (la ropa) to iron (the clothes)
planear to plan
planeta *m.* planet
planificación *f.* planning
plano city map
planta plant; floor (*of a building*) (*Sp.*)
plástico plastic; **botella de plástico** plastic bottle
plátano banana
plato plate; prepared dish; *pl.* dishes; **primer (segundo, tercer) plato** first (second, third) course
playa beach
plaza square, plaza
plazo term; **de corto/largo plazo** short/long term; **pagar (gu) a plazos** to pay in installments
pluma pen (P)
plumero feather duster
población *f.* population
poblado/a populated
pobre *adj.* poor
pobreza poverty; **umbral** (*m.*) **de la pobreza** poverty line

poco/a *adv.* little; *adj.* little; *pl.* few; **dentro de poco** in a little while; **un poco** a little

poder *m.* power

poder *irreg.* to be able to, can; **¿en qué puedo servirle?** how may I help you (*form. s.*)?; **¿me podría traer... ?** could you (*form. s.*) bring me . . . ?; **¿puedo probarme... ?** may I try on . . . ?

poema *m.* poem

poemario collection of poetry

poesía poetry

poeta *m., f.* poet

polémico/a controversial

policía *f.* police force; *m.* policeman; **mujer (f.) policía** policewoman

poliéster *m.* polyester

poliomielitis *f.* polio

politeísta *adj. m., f.* polytheist, believing in more than one god

política *s.* politics

político, mujer (f.) político politician

político/a political; **ciencias políticas** political science (P); **partido político** political party

pollo chicken

polvo *n.* dust; **quitar el polvo** to dust

poner *irreg.* to put; **poner alto el volumen** to turn the volume up high; **poner fin a** to end; **poner las cosas en orden** to put things in order; **ponerle los cuernos (a alguien)** to be unfaithful (to someone); **ponerle una inyección (a alguien)** to give (someone) a shot; **ponerse** to get, become (*emotion*); **ponerse de acuerdo** to come to an agreement; **ponérsele la piel de gallina a alguien** to get goosebumps

por for; because of; by, through, around; **estar** (*irreg.*) **por** + *inf.* to be about to + *inf.*; **llamar por teléfono** to call on the telephone; **pasar por la aduana** to go through customs; **por ciento** percent; **por dentro** within, (on the) inside; **por ejemplo** for example; **por favor** please; **por fin** finally; **por fuera** (on the) outside; **por la**

mañana/tarde/noche in the morning/afternoon/evening (night); **por lo menos** at least; **por primera vez** for the first time; **¿por qué?** why?; **por supuesto** of course

porcentaje *m.* percentage

porción *f.* **(de pastel, pizza)** slice (of cake, pizza)

porfiado/a persistent

porque because

portada home page (*Web*); cover (*book*)

portarse bien/mal to behave well/ badly

portátil portable; **computadora portátil** laptop computer; **estéreo portátil** portable stereo

portero/a doorperson; building manager

portugués *m.* Portuguese (*language*)

poseer (y) to possess

posesión *f.* possession

posesivo/a possessive

posgrado/a graduate; **estudios de posgrado** graduate studies

posibilidad *f.* possibility

posible possible

posición *f.* position

positivo/a positive

postre *m.* dessert

potable: agua (f. [*but* **el agua**]) **potable** drinking water

práctica *n.* practice

practicar (qu) to practice; **practicar el alpinismo de rocas** to rock climb; **practicar la escalada** to rappel; **practicar el paracaidismo** to skydive; **practicar el parapente** to hang glide; **practicar el yoga** to do yoga; **practicar un deporte** to practice a sport

pragmático/a pragmatic

precavido/a cautious

precio (fijo) (fixed) price; **estar** (*irreg.*) **a buen precio** to be a good price

precioso/a precious; valuable; **metales (m.) preciosos** precious metals

preciso/a precise; **es preciso** it's necessary

precolombino/a pre-Columbian (before Columbus)

predeterminado/a predetermined

predicción *f.* prediction

predominar to dominate

preferencia preference

preferir (ie, i) to prefer

pregunta *n.* question

preguntar to ask (questions)

preliminar preliminary

premio award; prize

prenda article of clothing

prender (las luces) to turn on (the lights)

prensa *n.* press

preocupación *f.* worry; concern

preocupado/a worried

preocuparse (por) to worry (about)

preparar to prepare

preparativo preparation

preparatoria high school

preposición *f.* preposition

presencia presence

presentación *f.* presentation; introduction (P)

presentador(a) anchorman, anchorwoman

presentar to present; to introduce; to show (*a film*)

presente *n. m., adj. m. f.* present (*time*)

preservar to preserve, maintain

presidencia presidency

presidencial presidential

presidente/a president

presión *f.* pressure; **presión arterial** blood pressure

presenciar to witness

prestado/a borrowed; **pedir (i, i) prestado/a** to borrow

préstamo *n.* loan; **sacar (qu) un préstamo** to take out a loan

prestar to loan, lend

presumido/a conceited

presupuesto (mensual) (monthly) budget

pretérito *gram.* preterite (tense)

pretexto pretext, excuse

prevalente prevalent

preventivo/a: señales (f. pl.) preventivas warning signs

previo/a previous
primaria: (escuela) primaria elementary school; **maestro/a de primaria** elementary school teacher
primavera spring (*season*)
primer, primero/a first; **por primera vez** for the first time; **primer (segundo, tercer) plato** first (second, third) course; **primera clase** first class
primo/a cousin; *pl.* cousins
principal *adj.* main, principal
principio beginning
prisa: tener (*irreg.*) **prisa** to be in a hurry
privacidad *f.* privacy
privado/a private; **casa privada** private residence; **con baño privado** with a private bath
privilegiado/a privileged
probabilidad *f.* probability
probable probable; **es probable** it's probable
probador *m.* dressing room
probar (ue) to try on; **¿puedo probarme… ?** may I try on . . . ?; **probarse** to try on
problema *m.* problem
problemático/a problematic
procesar to process
proceso process
producción *f.* production
producir *irreg.* to produce
producto product; **producto biodegradable** biodegradable product; **producto de limpieza** cleaning product; **producto desechable** disposable product; **producto farmacéutico** pharmaceutical product; **producto lácteo** dairy product; **producto nacional bruto** gross national product; **productos de exportación** export products
productor(a) producer
profesión *f.* profession
profesional *adj.* professional
profesor(a) professor (P)
profundo/a deep

programa *m.* program; **programa de entrevistas** talk show; **programa deportivo** sports show; **programa televisivo** television program
programación *f.* programming
programador(a) (computer) programmer
prohibir (prohíbo) to prohibit
prólogo prologue
promedio *n.* average
promesa promise; **cumplir las promesas** to keep one's word
prometer to promise
promiscuo/a promiscuous
pronombre *m.* pronoun
pronóstico del tiempo weather report
pronto soon; **tan pronto como** as soon as
pronunciación *f.* pronunciation
pronunciar to pronounce
propiedad *f.* property
propina tip; **dejar (una) propina** to leave a tip
propio/a own
proporcionar to give
propósito purpose; aim; intention; **a propósito** by the way
prosperidad *f.* prosperity
próspero/a prosperous
protección *f.* protection
proteger (j) to protect
proteína protein
protestar to protest
provecho: buen provecho enjoy your meal
provincia province, region
provocar (qu) to provoke
proximidad *f.* proximity
próximo/a next
prueba *n.* quiz, test
psicología psychology (P)
psicólogo/a psychologist
psiquiatra *m., f.* psychiatrist
publicación *f.* publication
publicar (qu) to publish
publicitario/a: anuncio publicitario commercial
público *n.* public; audience; **teléfono público** public telephone (P)
publico/a *adj.* public
pueblo small town

puerro leek
puerta door (P)
puerto (sea)port
puertorriqueño/a *n., adj.* Puerto Rican
pues… well . . .
puesto *n.* stand; **puesto que** given that
pulir to polish
pulmón *m.* lung
pulsar to click
punta de lanza spearhead
punto point; period; **en punto** on the dot (*time*); **punto de vista** point of view
puntual punctual; **ser** (*irreg.*) **puntual** to be punctual
puntualidad *f.* punctuality
puré (*m.*) **de papas** mashed potatoes
púrpura purple

Q

que that, which; than; **creer que** to think that; **hasta que** *conj.* until; **lo que** what, that which; **más + adj. + que** more + *adj.* + than; **tener** (*irreg.*) **que + inf.** to have to (*do something*)
¿qué? what?; **¿a qué hora… ?** at what time . . . ?, when . . . ?; **¿por qué?** why?; **¿qué carrera haces?** what's your (*fam. s.*) major (P); **¿qué clases tienes este semestre/trimestre?** what classes do you (*fam. s.*) have this semester/quarter? (P); **¿qué día es hoy?** what day is today?; **¿qué estudias?** what are you (*fam. s.*) studying? (P); **¿qué hora es?** what time is it?; **¿qué número calza?** what size shoe do you (*form. s.*) wear?; **¿qué trae… ?** what comes with . . . ?
quechua *m.* Quechua (*language*)
quedar to be located; **creo que le queda un poco grande** I think it's a bit big on you; **¿me queda bien?** does it fit me?; **quedarle bien/mal** to fit well/ poorly; **quedarse** to stay (*in a place*)
quehacer *m.* chore; **quehaceres domésticos** household chores

queja complaint
quejarse (de) to complain (about)
quemar to burn; **quemar calorías** to burn calories
querer *irreg.* to want; to love; **quiere decir** it means
queso cheese; **queso de crema** cream cheese
quien(es) who, whom
¿quién(es)? who? whom?
química chemistry (P)
químico / mujer (*f.*) **química** chemist
quince fifteen
quinientos/as five hundred
quinientos mil five hundred thousand
quiosco kiosk
quitar to remove, take away; **quitar el polvo** to dust; **quitarse** to take off (*clothing*)
quizá(s) perhaps

R

rabia rage; **darle** (*irreg.*) **rabia (a alguien)** to make (someone) angry
racismo racism
radio *f.* radio (*medium*)
rafting: hacer (*irreg.*) **rafting** to go rafting
raíz *f.* (*pl.* **raíces**) root; **bienes** (*m. pl.*) **raíces** real estate
ramo bouquet
rápido *adv.* fast
rápido/a *adj.* fast, quick; **comida rápida** fast food
raro/a strange; rare; **raras veces** infrequently, rarely
rascacielos *m. s.* skyscraper
rasgar (gu) to tear, rip
rasgo feature, trait
rasguñar to scratch
rato *n.* while, short time; **ratos libres** free time
ratón *m.* mouse (*animal*); mouse (*computer*)
raya stripe; **de rayas** striped; **mantenerse** (*like* **tener**) **a raya** to keep (*something*) away
rayo ray; **rayos X** X-rays
raza race (*people*)
razón *f.* reason

razonable reasonable
reacción *f.* reaction
reaccionar to react
real real; royal
realidad *f.* reality
realista *adj. m., f.* realistic
reality *m.* reality show (*TV*)
realizar (c) to attain, achieve
realmente really
rebaja sale
rebelde rebellious
recargable rechargeable; **pila recargable** rechargeable battery
recargar (gu) to recharge
recepción *f.* reception
recesión *f.* recession
receta recipe; prescription
recibir to receive
recibo receipt
reciclaje *m.* recycling
reciclar to recycle
recién recently; **recién nacido/a** newborn baby
reciente recent
recipiente *m.* container
recíproco/a reciprocal
recitar to recite
recoger (j) to pick up
recomendable recommendable
recomendación *f.* recommendation
recomendar (ie) to recommend
reconocer (zc) to recognize
reconocido/a renowned
recordar (ue) to remember
recorrido trip, journey
recorte *m.* clipping (*of a magazine*)
recreación *f.* recreation
recreo recess
recuerdo memory; souvenir; **comprar recuerdos** to buy souvenirs
recuperación *f.* recuperation
recuperarse to recuperate
recurrir a to turn to
recurso resource; **recursos naturales** natural resources
red *f.* net; Internet; **navegar (gu) la red** to surf the Web
redacción *f.* composition
reducir *irreg.* to reduce
reembolso reimbursement

reemplazar (c) to replace
reenviar (reenvío) to forward
referencia reference
referir(se) (ie, i) (a) to refer (to)
refinado/a refined
reflejar to reflect
reflexivo/a reflexive
refresco soft drink; **refresco dietético** diet soft drink
refrigerador *m.* refrigerator
regalar to give (*as a gift*)
regalo gift
regatear to bargain
regateo bargaining
régimen *m.* diet
región *f.* region
regresar to return (*to a place*); **regresar a casa** to go home
regulador(a) regulator
regular to regulate
reinado *n.* reign
reírse (i, i) to laugh
relación *f.* relationship
relacionado/a (con) related (to)
relacionarse to relate, be related to
relajado/a relaxed
relajante *adj.* relaxing
relajarse to relax
relatar to relate, tell
relato tale, story
religión *f.* religion
religioso/a religious
rellenar to fill
relleno/a (de) stuffed (with)
reloj *m.* clock (P); watch (P)
remar to row; **remar en canoa** to go canoeing
remedio remedy
remolino pinwheel
Renacimiento Renaissance
rencor *m.* anger; **guardar(le) rencor (a alguien)** to hold a grudge (against someone)
renovar (ue) to renew
renta per cápita per capita income
renunciar a to quit (*a job*); to give up
repartir to distribute
repasar to review
repaso review
repente: de repente suddenly
repetir (i, i) to repeat

repleto/a overflowing
reportaje *m.* report
reportar to report
reportero/a reporter
represa dam
representante *m., f.* representative
representar to represent
represivo/a repressive
reproductor (*m.*) **de CD/DVD/vídeo** CD/DVD/video player
república republic; **República Dominicana** Dominican Republic
requerir (ie, i) to require
requisito requirement
res *f.*: **carne** (*f.*) **de res** beef
resaltar to highlight
resentido/a resentful
reserva reserve; reservation (*hotel*)
reservación *f.* reservation
reservado/a reserved
resfriado *n.* cold (*sickness*); **tener** (*irreg.*) **un resfriado** to have a cold
resfriarse (me resfrío) to catch a cold
residencia estudiantil residence hall, dormitory (P)
resolución *f.* resolution
resolver (ue) (*p.p.* **resuelto/a**) **(conflictos)** to resolve (conflicts)
respectivo/a respective
respetar to respect; **respetar el espacio personal** to respect personal space
respeto respect
respetuoso/a respectful
respirar to breathe
responder to respond, answer
responsabilidad *f.* responsibility; **responsabilidad cívica** civic duty
responsable responsible
respuesta response, answer
restaurante *m.* restaurant; **cenar en un restaurante elegante** to eat in a fancy restaurant
resto rest, remainder; *pl.* remains; remnants
restricción *f.* restriction
resuelto/a (*p.p. of* **resolver**) resolved
resultado result
resultar to turn out, result
resumen *m.* summary

resumir to sum up
retirar to withdraw
retrasar to delay, retard
retroproyectora projector
reunión *f.* **(cívica)** (town) meeting
reunirse (me reúno) to get together
revelar to reveal
revisar to check, inspect
revista magazine
revolución *f.* revolution
revuelto/a (*p.p. of* **revolver**): **huevos revueltos** scrambled eggs
rey *m.* king; **Día** (*m.*) **de los Reyes Magos** Epiphany (January 6), Day of the Magi
rico/a rich, wealthy; delicious
ridículo/a ridiculous
rincón *m.* corner
riñón *m.* kidney
río river
ríoplatense *adj. pertaining to the* **río de la plata** (*Platte River*)
riqueza *s.* riches, wealth
ritmo rhythm
rito rite; ceremony
rivalidad *f.* rivalry
rizado/a curly; **pelo rizado** curly hair
robar to rob, steal
robo break-in
roca rock; **practicar (qu) el alpinismo de rocas** to rock climb
rodear to surround
rodilla knee
rogar (ue) (gu) to beg
rojo/a red
románico/a *adj.* Romance (*language*)
romántico/a romantic
romper (*p.p.* **roto/a**) to break; **romper con** to break up with; **romperse** to break (a bone)
roncar (qu) to snore
ronda *n.* round
ropa clothing
rosado/a pink
rosario rosary
rosbif *m.* roast beef
rosquilla bagel
rostro *n.* face
roto/a (*p.p. of* **romper**) broken
rozarse (c) con la gente to mingle with people

rubí *m.* ruby
rubio/a blond(e); **pelo rubio** blond hair
rueda wheel; **rueda de andar** treadmill; **rueda pinchada** flat tire
ruido noise
rumor *m.* rumor
ruso/a *n., adj.* Russian
ruta route

S

sábado Saturday
saber *irreg.* to know (*facts, information*); to find out (*about something*); **saber** + *inf.* to know how to (*do something*); **todavía no sé** I still don't know (P)
sabio/a wise
sabor *m.* taste, flavor
sabroso/a savory, tasty
sacar (qu) to take out; **sacar a pasear** to take for a walk; **sacar dinero** to withdraw money; **sacar fotos** to take pictures; **sacar la basura** to take out the trash; **sacar la lengua** to stick out one's tongue; **sacar la licencia de conducir** to get a driver's license; **sacar un préstamo** to take out a loan; **sacar un vídeo/DVD** to rent a video/DVD; **sacarle sangre** to draw blood
sacerdote *m.* priest
sacrificarse (qu) to sacrifice oneself
safari *m.* safari
sal *f.* salt
sala family room; **sala de clase** classroom (P); **sala de espera** waiting room
salado/a salty; **galleta salada** cracker
salchicha sausage
salida exit; way out
salir *irreg.* to leave; to go out; **¿a cuánto sale?** how much is it?; **salir a bailar** to go dancing; **salir con** to go out with
salsa salsa
saltar to jump; **saltar la cuerda** to jump rope

salto: hacer (*irreg.*) **el salto bungee** to bungee jump

salud *f.* health

saludable healthy

saludar to greet

saludo greeting

salvar to save

san *apocopated form of* **santo**

sandalia sandal

sándwich *m.* sandwich

sangre *f.* blood; **sacarle (qu) sangre** to draw blood

sanguíneo/a *adj.* blood

santería *religion of African origin practiced in the Caribbean*

santo/a *n., adj.* saint

se *refl. pron.* herself, himself, itself, yourself (*form. s.*), themselves, yourselves (*form. pl.*)

se alquila for rent

secadora dryer

sección *f.* section

seco/a dry

secreto *n.* secret; **ocultar(lo) secretos (a alguien)** to hide secrets (from someone)

secundario/a secondary; **escuela secundaria** high school; **maestro/a de secundaria** high school teacher

seda silk

sedentario/a sedentary

sediento/a thirsty

seducir (zc) to seduce

seductor(a) seductive

seguida: en seguida right away

seguir (i, i) (g) to follow; **seguir derecho** to continue straight ahead

según according to

segundo/a *adj.* second; **segundo plato** second course

seguramente surely

seguridad *f.* safety; **pasar por seguridad** to go through security

seguro insurance; **seguro antirrobo** antitheft insurance; **seguro contra incendios** fire insurance; **seguro de automóvil** automobile insurance; **seguro de vida** life insurance; **seguro de vivienda**

homeowner's insurance; **seguro médico** medical insurance

seguro/a *adj.* sure; safe; **estar** (*irreg.*) **seguro/a de** to be sure of

seis six

seiscientos/as six hundred

seiscientos mil six hundred thousand

selección *f.* selection; national team (*soccer*)

seleccionar to select, choose

sello seal, stamp

selva (tropical) (tropical) jungle

semáforo signal; traffic light

semana week; **fin** (*m.*) **de semana** weekend; **semana entrante** next week; **semana pasada** last week

semanal weekly

semejante similar

semejanza similarity

semestre *m.* semester

semilla seed

senador(a) senator

sencillo/a simple; **cama sencilla** twin (single) bed

sendero path

seno breast (*of a person*)

sensación *f.* sensation

sensacionalista *m., f.* sensationalist

sensible sensitive

sentarse (ie) to sit down

sentido *n.* sense; **sentido de dirección** sense of direction; **sentido del humor** sense of humor

sentimental sentimental

sentimiento feeling, emotion

sentir (ie, i) to feel; **sentirse** to feel (*emotion, health*); **sentirse** + *adj., adv* to feel + *adj., adv.*

señal *f.* sign; signal; **señales preventivas** warning signs

señalar to point out

señor (Sr.) man; Mr.

señora (Sra.) woman; Mrs.

señorita (Srta.) young woman; Miss, Ms.

separación *f.* separation

separado/a separated

septentrional northern

septiembre September

ser *irreg.* to be (P); **¿cómo es?** what is he/she/it/like? what are you (*form. s.*) like?; **¿cuál es su apellido?** what's his/her last name? (P); **¿cuál es tu apellido?** what's your (*fam. s.*) last name? (P); **¿de dónde eres?** where are you (*fam. s.*) from (P); **era** he/she/it was, you (*form. s.*) were; **es buena idea; es de...** it's made of . . .; **es imposible** it's impossible; **es la una** it's one o'clock; **es necesario** it's necessary; **es preciso** it's necessary; **es probable** it's probable; **mi apellido es...** my last name is . . . (P); **mi nombre es...** my name is . . . (P); **parece ser** it seems to be; he/she seems . . .; **pasar a ser** to become; **¿qué hora es?** what time is it?; **ser aficionado/a** to be a fan; **(no) ser de fiar** to be (un)reliable; **ser hábil para (las matemáticas, las ciencias)** to be good at (math, science); **ser parcial** to be biased; **ser peletero/a** to be a kiss-up; **ser puntual** to be punctual; **son de...** they're made of . . .; **soy de...** I'm from . . . (P)

serie *f.* series

serio/a serious

serpiente *f.* snake

servicio service; **servicio de cuarto** room service; **servicios médicos** medical services; **servicios sociales** social services

servilleta napkin

servir (i, i) to serve; **¿en qué puedo servirle?** how may I help you?; **servir de compañía** to give, keep company

sesenta sixty

sesión *f.* session

setecientos/as seven hundred

setecientos mil seven hundred thousand

setenta seventy

sexo sex

si if

sí yes; **sí, por supuesto** yes, of course

SIDA (síndrome [*m.*] **de inmunodeficiencia adquirida)** AIDS (Acquired Immune Deficiency Syndrome)

siempre always

siesta nap; **echar una siesta** to take a nap

siete seven

siglo century; **siglo XXI** twenty-first century

significado meaning

significar (qu) to mean

significativamente significantly

signo *n.* sign (*horoscope*)

siguiente following; next

silencioso/a silent, quiet

silla chair (P)

sillón *m.* armchair

simbolizar (c) to symbolize

símbolo symbol

simbología symbology

similitud *f.* similarity

simpático/a friendly, nice

sin without; **sin duda** without a doubt; **sin embargo** *conj.* however; **sin que** without

sincero/a sincere

sincretismo syncretism, consolidation of different religious doctrines

síndrome *m.* syndrome; **síndrome de inmunodeficiencia adquirida (SIDA)** Acquired Immune Deficiency Syndrome (AIDS)

sino but (rather)

sinónimo synonym

sinopsis *f.* synopsis

síntoma *m.* symptom

sinuoso/a winding

siquiera: ni siquiera not even

sistema *m.* system; **analista** (*m., f.*) **de sistemas** systems analyst

sitio place, location; site; **diseñador(a) de sitios** Web site designer

situación *f.* situation

situado/a situated, located

sobras *pl.* leftovers

sobre about; on, on top of

sobresaliente excellent

sobrino/a nephew, niece

sociable sociable

social social; **ciencias sociales** social sciences (P); **servicios sociales** social services; **trabajador(a) social** social worker

sociedad *f.* society

socio/a associate; partner

socioeconómico/a socioeconomic

sociolingüístico/a sociolinguistic

sociología sociology (P)

sofá *m.* sofa

sofisticado/a sophisticated

soja soy(bean)

sol *m.* sun; **hace sol** it's sunny; **tomar el sol** to sunbathe

solamente only

solas: a solas alone

soldado, mujer (*f.*) **soldado** soldier

soler (ue) + *inf.* to be in the habit of / be accustomed to (*doing something*)

sólido/a solid

solitario/a solitary

sólo (solamente) *adv.* only; **sólo estoy mirando** I'm just looking

solo/a alone

soltero/a single, unmarried; **madre** (*f.*) **soltera** single mother; **padre** (*m.*) **soltero** single father

solución *f.* solution

solucionar to solve

sombrero hat

sonar (ue) to ring

soneto sonnet

sonreír (i, i) to smile

sonrisa smile

sonrojarse to blush

soñador(a) dreamer

soñar (ue) (con) to dream (about)

sopa soup

soplo breeze; breath

soporte *m.* support

sorprendente surprising

sorprender to surprise

sorpresa surprise; **fiesta de sorpresa** surprise party

sospechar to suspect

sospechoso/a suspicious

sostener (*like* **tener**) to hold up, support

sótano basement

su(s) *poss.* his, her, its, their, your (*form. s., pl.*); **¿cuál es su apellido?** what's his/her last name? (P)

subdivisión *f.* subdivision; subsection

subida rise

subir to rise, go up; **subir a** to board; **subirse a los árboles** to climb trees

subjuntivo *gram.* subjunctive (mood)

sublevarse to revolt

subrayar to underline

suburbio suburb

suceder to happen

sucesión *f.* succession

suceso event, happening

sucio/a dirty

sudadera sweatshirt

Sudamérica South America

sudamericano/a *n., adj.* South American

sudar to sweat

suegro/a father-in-law, mother-in-law

sueldo (mínimo) (minimum) wage, salary

suelo floor

sueño *n.* dream; **tener** (*irreg.*) **sueño** to be sleepy

suerte *f.* luck; **tener** (*irreg.*) **suerte** to be lucky

suéter *m.* sweater

suficiente sufficient, enough

sufrir to suffer

sugerencia suggestion

sugerir (ie, i) to suggest

suicidio suicide

sujeto *n.* subject

sumar to add

superar to exceed

supermercado supermarket

supuesto/a (*p.p. of* **suponer**) supposed; **por supuesto** of course

sur *m.* south; **al sur de** to the south of

surfear to surf

suroeste *m.* southwest

suspender to suspend

sustancia substance

sustancial substantial

sustantivo noun

sustentable: desarrollo sustentable sustainable development
sustitución *f.* substitution
sustituir (y) to substitute
suyo/a/os/as *poss.* your, of yours (*form. s., pl.*); his, of his; her, of hers

T

tabaco tobacco
tacaño/a greedy, stingy
tacón *m.* heel (*shoe*); **zapatos de tacón alto** high-heeled shoes
tal such, such a; **con tal de que** *conj.* provided that; **¿qué tal?** how's it going?; **tal vez** perhaps
talento talent
talentoso/a talented
talla size (*clothes*); **¿cuál es su talla?** what size do you (*form. s.*) wear?
tamaño size; **¿de qué tamaño es… ?** what size is … ?
también also, too
tampoco neither, not either
tan so; **tan… como** as … as; **tan pronto como** as soon as
tanto *adv.* so much
tanto/a *adj.* so much; such; *pl.* so many; **tanto/a/os/as… como** as much/many … as
tapada: tener (*irreg.*) **la nariz tapada** to have a stuffed-up nose
tarántula tarantula
tardar to take time (*to do something*)
tarde *n. f.* afternoon, evening; **buenas tardes** good afternoon/evening (P); **de la tarde** in the afternoon, evening (P.M.); **por la tarde** in the afternoon/evening
tarde *adv.* late
tarea homework; task
tarifa rate, price, fare
tarjeta card; **tarjeta de crédito** credit card; **tarjeta de felicitación** greeting card
tasa rate, level; **tasa de desempleo** unemployment rate
taxista *m., f.* taxi driver
taza cup (*coffee*)
tazón *m.* bowl

te *d.o.* you (*fam. s.*); *i.o.* to/for you (*fam. s.*); *refl. pron.* yourself (*fam. s.*); **¿cómo te llamas?** what is your (*fam. s.*) name? (P); **te gusta…** you (*fam. s.*) like …
té (*m.*) **(caliente/helado)** (hot/iced) tea
teatro theater
teclado keyboard
técnica technique
técnico/a *n.* technician; *adj.* technical
tecnología technology
tecnológico/a technological
tejido/a woven
telefónica telephone company
teléfono telephone; **llamar por teléfono** to call on the telephone; **teléfono celular** cell phone; **teléfono público** public telephone (P)
telenovela soap opera
telepático/a telepathic
televidente *m., f.* television viewer
televisión *f.* television (*medium*); **canal** (*m.*) **de televisión** television channel; **ver** (*irreg.*) **la televisión** to watch TV
televisivo/a *adj.* television, **programa** (*m.*) **televisivo** television program
televisor *m.* television (*set*) (P)
tema *m.* theme, topic
temer to fear
temperatura temperature; **tomar(le) la temperatura** to take (*someone's*) temperature
temporada season (*sports*)
temprano early
tendencia tendency
tender (ie) to tend to
tenedor *m.* fork
tener *irreg.* to have; **tener… años** to be … years old; **tener celos** to be jealous; **tener don de gentes** to have a way with people; **tener éxito** to be successful; **tener expectativas** to have expectations; **tener fiebre** to have a fever; **tener ganas de** + *inf.* to feel like (*doing something*); **tener hambre** to be hungry; **tener la nariz tapada** to

have a stuffed-up nose; **tener prisa** to be in a hurry; **tener que** + *inf.* to have to (*do something*); **tener sueño** to be sleepy; **tener suerte** to be lucky; **tener un resfriado** to have a cold; **tenerle cariño a alguien** to be fond of someone; **tenerle envidia (a alguien)** to be envious (of someone); **tenerle miedo (a alguien)** to be afraid (of someone); **tengo una clase de…** I have a(n) … class (P); **¿tiene Ud. la hora?** do you (*form. s.*) have the time?
tenis *m.* tennis; **cancha de tenis** tennis court; **zapatos de tenis** tennis shoes
tensión *f.* tension; **tensión arterial** blood pressure
tenso/a tense; stressed
tentación *f.* temptation
terapeuta *m., f.* therapist
tercer, tercero/a third; **tercer plato** third course
terco/a stubborn
terminación *f.* ending
terminar to finish
término term
termostato thermostat
terraza terrace
terremoto earthquake
terrenos *pl.* lands
terrestre terrestrial
territorio territory
terrorismo terrorism
terrorista *n. m., f.* terrorist
testigo *n. m., f.* witness
testimonio testimony
textiles *m., pl.* textiles
texto text; **libro de texto** textbook
ti *obj. of prep.* you (*fam. s.*)
tibio/a warm
tiburón *m.* shark
tiempo weather, time; **a tiempo** on time; **¿cuánto tiempo hace que… ?** how long has it been since … ? **hace buen/mal tiempo** it's good/bad weather; **hace (mucho) tiempo** (a long time) ago; **llegar (gu) a tiempo** to arrive on time; **pasar (mucho) tiempo** to spend (a lot of)

time; **pérdida de tiempo** waste of time; **pronóstico del tiempo** weather report

tienda store, shop

tierra earth, land

tijeras *pl.* scissors

timbre *m.* bell; ring (*tone*)

tímido/a timid

tinto/a: vino tinto red wine

tío/a uncle, aunt; *pl.* aunts and uncles

típico/a typical

tipo type; **tipos de interés** interest rates

tiras cómicas comics; cartoons

tirar to throw out

titular *m.* headline

titularse to be titled

título title

tiza chalk (P)

toalla (de papel) (paper) towel

tocar (qu) (el piano / la guitarra) to play (the piano / the guitar); to touch

tocino bacon

todavía still, yet; **todavía no sé** I still don't know (P)

todo/a all; every; **todas las noches** every night; **todos los días** every day

tolerante tolerant

tomar to take; to drink; **tomar apuntes** to take notes; **tomar café** to drink coffee; **tomar cerveza** to drink beer; **tomar el sol** to sunbathe; **tomar una clase** to take a class; **tomar(le) la temperatura** to take (*someone's*) temperature; **tomarse algo muy a pecho** to take something to heart; to feel something intensely

tomate *m.* tomato

tono tone

tontería foolish thing

tonto/a silly, foolish

topacio topaz

torbellino whirlwind

tormentoso/a stormy

toronja grapefruit

torpe clumsy

torre *f.* tower

torta cake

tortilla (de maíz) *thin cake made of cornmeal or flour*; **tortilla española** *omelette made of eggs, potatoes, and onions* (*Sp.*)

tortuga turtle

tos *f.* cough; **jarabe** (*m.*) **para la tos** cough syrup

tostada de pan a la francesa French toast

tostado/a toasted; **pan** (*m.*) **tostado** toast

trabajador(a) *adj.* hardworking; *n.* worker; **trabajador(a) social** social worker

trabajar to work; **trabajar en equipo** to work as a team

trabajo job; **Día** (*m.*) **del Trabajo** Labor Day

trabársele la lengua a alguien to get tongue-tied

tradicional traditional; **pérdida de valores tradicionales** loss of traditional values

traducir (*like* **conducir**) to translate

traer *irreg.* to bring; **¿me podría traer… ?** could you (*form. s.*) bring me . . . ? **¿qué trae… ?** what comes with . . . ?

tráfico traffic

tragedia tragedy

traicionar to betray

traje *m.* suit; **traje de baño** bathing suit

trama plot (*of a story*)

tranquilo/a calm, peaceful

transacción *f.* transaction

transición *f.* transition

tránsito traffic

transmitir to transmit

transparente transparent

transporte *m.* transportation

trapo rag

tras *adv.* behind

tratado treaty; **Tratado de Libre Comercio (TLC)** North America Free Trade Agreement (NAFTA)

tratamiento treatment

tratar to treat; to deal with; **tratarse de** to be about

través: a través de through, by means of

travieso/a mischievous

trece thirteen

treinta thirty; **los años treinta** the thirties

treinta y dos thirty-two

treinta y uno thirty-one

tren *m.* train; **estación** (*f.*) **del tren** train station

tres three

tres mil three thousand

trescientos/as three hundred

trescientos mil three hundred thousand

trimestre *m.* quarter (*school*)

triste sad

triunfo triumph

tropical: selva tropical tropical jungle

trotar to jog

trozo piece, chunk

truco trick; **hacer** (*irreg.*) **trucos** to do tricks

tú *sub. pron.* you (*fam. s.*) (P)

tu(s) *poss.* your (*fam. s.*); **¿cuál es tu apellido?** what's your (*fam. s.*) last name? (P)

tumultuoso/a tumultuous

turista *n. m., f.* tourist

turístico/a *adj.* tourist; **clase** (*f.*) **turística** tourist class

tutearse to address each other as **tú**

tuyo/a/os/as *poss.* your, of yours (*fam. s.*)

U

u or (*used instead of* **o** *before words beginning with* **o** *or* **ho**)

ubicación *f.* location

ubicado/a located

último/a last

umbral (*m.*) **de la pobreza** poverty line

un, uno/a *indef. art.* a, an; one (P); *pl.* some, any; **a la una** at one o'clock; **es la una** it's one o'clock; **un poco de** a little (of) (P); **una vez al mes** once a month

único/a only; **hijo/a único/a** only child
unión f. union
universidad f. university (P)
universitario/a of or pertaining to the university
uno one; **cada uno** each one
urbano/a urban
uruguayo/a n., adj. Uruguayan
usar to use; to wear (clothing)
uso n. use
usted (Ud.) sub. pron. you (form. s.) (P); obj. of prep. you (form. s.)
ustedes (Uds.) sub. pron. you (form. pl.) (P); obj. of prep. you (form. pl.)
usuario/a user
útil useful
utilizar (c) to utilize, use
uva grape

V

vaca cow
vacación f. vacation; **de vacaciones** on vacation
vacío/a empty
vainilla vanilla
Valentín: Día (m.) **de San Valentín** St. Valentine's Day
válido/a valid
valiente brave
valle m. valley
valor m. value; **Bolsa de valores** stock market; **pérdida de valores tradicionales** loss of traditional values
valorar to value
vano/a vain
vapor steam; **al vapor** steamed
vaqueros jeans
variación f. variation
variar (varío) to vary
variedad f. variety
varios/as pl. various
vasco: País (m.) **Vasco** Basque country
vaso glass (water)
vecindad f. neighborhood
vecindario neighborhood
vecino/a neighbor
vegetal m. vegetable

vegetariano/a vegetarian
vehículo vehicle
veinte twenty; **los años veinte** the twenties
veinticinco twenty-five
veinticuatro twenty-four
veintidós twenty-two
veintinueve twenty-nine
veintiocho twenty-eight
veintiséis twenty-six
veintisiete twenty-seven
veintitrés twenty-three
veintiún, veintiuno/a twenty-one
velo veil
velocidad f. speed
vendaje m. bandage
vendedor(a) salesperson; vendor
vender to sell
vengativo/a vengeful
venir irreg. to come
venta sale; **de venta** for sale
ventaja advantage
ventana window (P)
ver irreg. (p.p. **visto/a**) to see; **nos vemos** see you around; **ver la televisión** to watch TV; **ver un espectáculo** to see a show; **ver una película** to watch a movie
verano summer
veras: de veras really
verbo verb
verdad f. truth
verdadero/a true
verde green; unripe; **judías verdes** green beans
verdura vegetable
vergüenza shame
verificar (qu) to check, verify
verso line (of poetry)
vestido n. dress
vestir (i, i) to dress; **vestirse** to get dressed
veterano/a veteran
veterinario/a veterinarian; **llevar al / a la veterinario/a** to take to the veterinarian
vez f. (pl. **veces**) times; **a veces** sometimes; **cada vez** each time; **cada vez más** more and more; **de vez en cuando** once in a while; **la**

próxima vez the next time; **la última vez** the last time; **muchas veces** often; **pagar (gu) de una vez** to pay off all at once; **raras veces** infrequently, rarely; **tal vez** perhaps; **una vez (al mes)** once (a month)
vía way; path; **país** (m.) **en vías de desarrollo** developing country
viajar to travel, take a trip
viaje m. trip; **agencia de viajes** travel agency; **agente** (m., f.) **de viajes** travel agent; **hacer** (irreg.) **un viaje** to take a trip
viajero/a traveler; **cheque** (m.) **de viajero** traveler's check
vida life; **seguro de vida** life insurance
vídeo video; **reproductor** (m.) **de vídeo** video player; **sacar (qu) un vídeo** to rent a video
videocámara camcorder
videojuego video game; **jugar (ue) (gu) a los videojuegos** to play video games
vidrio glass; **botella de vidrio** glass bottle
viejo/a n. elderly person; **Noche** (f.) **Vieja** New Year's Eve
viento wind; **hace (mucho) viento** it's (very) windy
viernes m. inv. Friday
vigilar to watch (over); to supervise
villano/a villain; antagonist
vino wine; **degustar vinos** to go wine tasting; **vino blanco** white wine; **vino tinto** red wine
viña vineyard
violencia violence; **violencia doméstica** domestic violence
violento/a violent; **crimen** (m.) **violento** violent crime
virtud f. virtue
visitar to visit; **visitar a la familia** to visit one's family; **visitar un museo** to visit a museum
víspera eve; day before
vista view; **punto de vista** point of view
vistazo glance; **echar un vistazo** to look over

vitalicio/a for life
viudo/a widowed; widower, widow
vivienda housing; **seguro de vivienda** homeowner's insurance
vivir to live
vivo/a alive
vocabulario vocabulary
vocal *f.* vowel
volante *m.* steering wheel
volar (ue) to fly
volcán *m.* volcano
volcánico/a volcanic
vólibol *m.* volleyball
volumen *m.* volume; **bajar el volumen** to lower the volume; **poner** (*irreg.*) **alto el volumen** to turn the volume up high
voluntario/a volunteer; **trabajar de voluntario/a** to volunteer
volver (ue) (*p.p.* **vuelto/a**) to return (*to a place*); **volver a** + *inf.* to (*do something*) again
vos *fam. s.* you (*used instead of* **tú** *in certain countries of Central and South America*)

vosotros/as *sub. pron.* you (*fam. pl. Sp.*) (P); *obj. of prep.* you (*fam. pl. Sp.*)
votante *m., f.* voter
votar to vote
voto: derecho al voto right to vote
voz *f.* (*pl.* **voces**) voice; **en voz alta** aloud
vuelo (directo) (direct) flight; **asistente** (*m., f.*) **de vuelo** flight attendant
vuelta *n.* turn; **dar** (*irreg.*) **la vuelta a** to go around (*something*); **de ida y vuelta** *adj.* round-trip
vuelto/a (*p.p. of* **volver**) returned
vuestro/a/os/as *poss.* your (*fam. pl. Sp.*), of yours (*fam. pl. Sp.*)

W

web Web (World Wide Web); **página web** Web page

X

X: rayos X X-rays

Y

y and (P); **y cuarto** quarter past (*hour*); **y media** half past (*hour*)
ya already; **ya murió** he/she already died; **ya no** no longer
yeso cast (*for a broken bone*)
yo *sub. pron.* I (P)
yoga *m.* yoga; **practicar (qu) el yoga** to do yoga
yogur *m.* yogurt

Z

zanahoria carrot
zapatería shoe store
zapatilla slipper
zapato shoe; **zapatos de cuero** leather shoes; **zapatos de tacón alto** high-heeled shoes; **zapatos de tenis** tennis shoes
zapping: hacer (*irreg.*) **zapping** to channel surf
zona zone
zumo juice (*Sp.*)